Kids' Cookbook

Kids' Cookbook

Bridget Jones

GALLERY BOOKS
An imprint of W.H. Smith Publishers Inc.
112 Madison Avenue
New York, New York 10016

A QUINTET BOOK
produced for GALLERY BOOKS
An imprint of W.H. Smith Publishers Inc.
112 Madison Avenue
New York, New York 10016

ISBN 0-8317-1759-9

This book was designed and produced by
Quintet Publishing Limited
6 Blundell Street
London N7 9BH

Creative Director: Peter Bridgewater
Designer and Illustrator: Sally McKay
Editor: Barbara Fuller
Photographer: Ian Howes

Typeset in Great Britain by
Central Southern Typesetters, Eastbourne
Manufactured in Hong Kong by
Regent Publishing Services Limited
Printed in Hong Kong
by Kwong Fat Offset Printing Company Limited

CONTENTS

Before You Start   6

Cooking For Fun   11

It's Simple to Start Cooking   22

Real Meals   34

Fast Foods   50

Throwing a Party   63

A Gift From The Cook   88

BEFORE YOU START

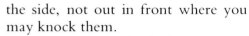

Cooking is fun. To make sure you enjoy cooking and the food tastes good enough to eat, read through these notes first.

★ Always ask if you can cook.
★ Make sure you have an adult in the kitchen to help.
★ Put an apron on to keep your clothes clean. Having an apron on also keeps your clothes away from the food and the cooker.
★ Keep long sleeves rolled up out of the way.
★ Wash your hands really well in hot soapy water.
★ Read through the recipe first.
★ Find all the ingredients and put them ready.
★ Set out all the utensils.
★ Keep a clean, damp dishtowel near to wipe up any mess.

Now you may begin!

the side, not out in front where you may knock them.
★ Always watch food which is cooking under the broiler.
★ As soon as you have finished cooking food turn off the heat.
★ Take extra care when using knives. Make sure the knife is the right size so you can hold it properly.
★ Keep your fingers out of the way when cutting and chopping. Cut slowly to get it right.
★ Always wash your knife and scrub the board after cutting raw fish, meat or chicken and before cutting up any other ingredients.
★ Keep the countertop clean by wiping up as you are cooking.
★ If you spill anything wipe it up at once.
★ Don't forget to wash up and clean up the kitchen!

SAFE AND CLEAN

Remember that what you are cooking is going to be eaten. The food must be kept clean all the time. If you have an accident while you are cooking, there will not be any food to eat. So always remember the S + C Rules.

★ Make sure you have an adult near when you are using the stovetop, broiler or oven.
★ Always use pot holders when you are handling hot dishes.
★ Put a heatproof mat on the work surface before taking hot pans and dishes from the stovetop, broiler or oven.
★ When you put pans on the stovetop make sure the handles are pointing to

USING THE MICROWAVE

The microwave oven is safe to use because it is not as hot as the stovetop or oven. You must remember to use it properly.

★ Never put baking pans, cooking foil or wire bag ties in the microwave.
★ Never switch the microwave on without any food in it.
★ Take care when setting the timer. Check that you have the right cooking time.
★ Check that you are using the correct power setting.
★ Always cook food for a short time. Take it out and stir or turn the food before cooking again for another short time.

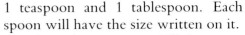

★ Remember that the food gets very hot. Use pot holders to take dishes from the microwave.

★ When you think the food is cooked, check that it is cooked through. Stir wet foods before serving. If parts of the food are cold or not cooked, then put it back in the microwave and cook for another short time.

★ There are microwave notes for some of the recipes. The times are for a 650 watt oven. Ask what power your microwave cooks at and check that it is the same. If it has a lower power, the cooking will take a little longer. If it has a higher power the food will cook more quickly.

WEIGHING AND MEASURING INGREDIENTS

WEIGHTS

Packaged food is measured by weight. Vegetables and other fresh foods are bought by weight. Always check the quantity on the package of food.

CUPS

Most of the ingredients are measured in cups. All cups of food should be level, not heaped. The food should be shaken down into the cup but not packed tight. Some quantities include a 'scant' volume, in which case the cup should only just be full, with the ingredients slightly below the rim.

★ Use a knife to level dry ingredients across the top of the cup.

★ Make sure to stand the cup on a level surface when measuring liquids.

MEASURING TEASPOONS AND TABLESPOONS

When a recipe tells you to add 1 teaspoon of something, or 2 tablespoons, you must use proper measuring spoons.

★ Measuring spoons come in small sets. They include ¼ teaspoon, ½ teaspoon,

1 teaspoon and 1 tablespoon. Each spoon will have the size written on it.

★ Use the right size spoon. Fill the spoon with the ingredient. Use a knife to level the top of the spoon when measuring dry ingredients.

★ Hold the spoon steady and level for a few seconds when measuring liquid to check that it is full.

WHAT IS A ...
KITCHEN KNIFE

For cutting up and for chopping food you will need a sharp kitchen knife, also called a chef's knife. Make sure it is not too big to handle.

SPATULA OR BLUNT KNIFE

This is a knife with a rounded end. It does not have a sharp edge. Some dinner knives are blunt so they may be used instead of a spatula. A spatula is used to lift cookies off cookie sheets or to spread butter, frosting or soft cheese.

CHOPPING BOARD

When you cut something always use a chopping board. Make sure the board is safe and firm on the countertop. If the surface is slippery, put a piece of paper towel under the board. Plastic boards are more advisable than wooden ones because they are easier to clean. When you have finished cooking you must scrub the chopping board with a brush and kitchen cleaner.

GRATER

There are lots of different types. They have fine or coarse blades. Always take care when grating food – it is easy to grate the end of your fingers and it hurts!

LEMON SQUEEZER

Some recipes tell you to squeeze the juice from a lemon or orange. You have to cut the fruit in half, then hold one half on a lemon squeezer. Twist the fruit around, pressing it down on the squeezer to get all the juice out.

WHISK

This is used for beating eggs and for whipping cream. A hand whisk is made up of wire loops and a handle. A hand-held rotary whisk has two metal whisks that are turned by you turning a handle. An electric beater is very quick but you should never use one unless you have an adult with you.

STRAINER

This is used for sifting flour that may be lumpy. It is also used for making a purée, or paste, out of food. Stand the strainer over a bowl before putting food in it.

COLANDER

A bowl with holes in it. This is used to drain food. Cooked pasta is drained in a colander. Shredded cabbage or lettuce may be put in a colander to drain when it has been washed. Always put the colander in the sink or over a bowl.

COOKIE SHEET

A flat metal tray used for baking cookies and other foods in the oven. Sometimes a cookie sheet is covered with paper or plastic wrap and used to put delicate foods on while they are chilling or setting.

WIRE RACK

This is used to cool hot food. Wire racks may be round, square or oblong. Some cakes and cookies become soggy underneath if they are not put on a rack to cool.

PASTRY BAG

A tough bag made of plastic or material. The bag has a pointed end with a small hole in it. You put a tip in the hole, then fill the bag with cream or other food. When you fold the ends of the bag together and squeeze, the food comes out.

TIP

There are lots of different tips. Tiny tips are used to decorate cakes. Very big tips are used to pipe mashed potato into swirls. Medium sized tips are used for piping whipped cream on cakes.

PASTRY BRUSH

This is a small brush made for kitchen use. A pastry brush is used for brushing pastry and other foods with egg, milk or water. After you have grated fruit rind, use a pastry brush to brush all the peel off the grater.

HOW TO . . .
CHOP AN ONION

Chop the ends off the onion.

Peel the onion.

Cut into thin slices.

Chop the slices into small pieces.

HEATPROOF MAT

Before you take a hot pan or cooking container off the stovetop or from the oven, place a heatproof mat on the countertop. This is so the countertop doesn't get scorched.

CLEAN MUSHROOMS

1 Cut off the ends of the mushroom stems.
2 Mushrooms must not be put into a bowl of water. Rinse them one at a time under cold running water. Hold the mushroom like an umbrella under the water, with the stem down and the rounded side up.
3 Rub any dirt off the rounded side with your fingers. Shake the water off the mushroom. Put the mushroom with the stem up on double thickness paper towels. Pat it dry.

MAKE BREADCRUMBS

1 Cut the crusts off a piece of bread.
2 Rub the bread on the coarse side of a grater, letting the crumbs fall into a bowl.
3 If you have a blender or food processor, then ask an adult if they will make some bread crumbs for you in that.

RUB FAT INTO FLOUR

1 Use a knife to cut the fat into small pieces.
2 Wash and dry your hands in cold water. If your hands are warm the fat will become very sticky.
3 Use just the tips of your fingers to pick up a lump of fat and some flour. Lift it slightly above the mixture.
4 Rub the fat and flour together between your thumb and fingertips. Let the mixture fall back into the bowl.
5 The mixture is ready when there are not any large lumps of fat. It should look like fresh breadcrumbs.

SEPARATE AN EGG

Tap the egg in the middle to break the shell. Pull the shell lightly apart with your thumbs. Let the white run

into the bowl and keep the yolk in the shell.

Open the shell into two pieces. Keep the yolk in one half. Pour the white

from each half into the bowl. Tip the yolk into a second bowl.

FILL A PIPING BAG

1 Put the tip in the bag.
2 Put the tip end of the bag in a measuring cup and fold the rest of the bag down around the outside of the cup.
3 Use a spoon to put the cream in the bag.
4 Gather up the ends of the bag and twist them together.

PIPE CREAM

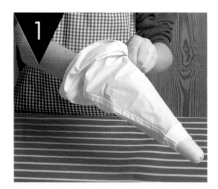

Put the nozzle in the piping bag.

Put the nozzle end in a measuring jug. Fold the bag around the jug.

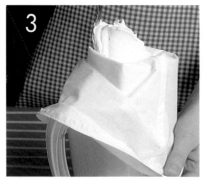

Put the cream in the bag using a spoon.

Hold the nozzle just above what you want to pipe and squeeze the bag to push out the cream.

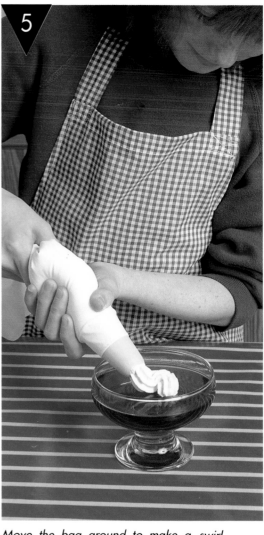

Move the bag around to make a swirl.

▶·*M*arzipan·◀

*1 cup ground almonds
5 tablespoons confectioner's sugar
4 tablespoons superfine sugar
1 egg yolk
a drop of almond flavouring*

Makes 1 bag

Put the almonds in a bowl. Stir in the confectioner's sugar and the superfine sugar.

Add the egg yolk and almond flavouring. Mix the ingredients with a spoon until they begin to stick. Wash and dry your hands, then press the mixture together to make a ball of paste. Knead the paste by pressing it flat with the palm of your hand, then squeezing it into a ball. Do this until smooth.

A NOTE TO ADULTS

The recipes in this book include some that are very simple and others that are more suitable for older children. Always supervise young children when they are cooking. Encourage your children to cook but always make sure they ask to use the kitchen so you know what they are doing. If they are preparing food that involves using the stove, oven or broiler, then stay with them. No matter what age, always check what they are doing, which foods they are using, the utensils and the results.

COOKING FOR FUN

⊫·Crazy Crackers·◂⫶

Make these using other ingredients — try using pieces of cooked ham or salami, small pieces of red or green pepper, cut up small pickled gherkins or use sliced celery sticks. Have fun making lots of different patterns or try these ideas.

1 To make the boats, spread the cream cheese on 4 crackers and make small peaks in it to look like waves. Cut 8 small triangles out of the cheese slice to look like sails. Cut the tomato slices in half.

2 Put a piece of tomato on each cracker to look like the bottom of the boat and put the cheese triangles above the tomatoes to look like sails. Leave a little space all around the sails. Put strips of cucumber between the sails to make masts and add a small triangle of cucumber peel to look like a flag.

3 For the faces, mix the catchup with the cream cheese and spread it on 4 crackers. Break the potato sticks and put them on the crackers to look like hair. Add 2 raisins to each to look like eyes. Cut the radishes into quarters. Put 1 piece of radish in the middle of the face to look like a nose, making sure the red skin is facing up. Turn the other wedges of radish on their sides and place on the crackers to look like mouths.

4 To make the flowers, mix the cream cheese with the parsley and spread it on 4 crackers. Use a small flower-shaped cookie cutter or small round cookie cutter to cut 4 pieces out of the cheese. Put 1 on each cracker.

5 Cut a thin strip from the middle of each cucumber slice and put these on the crackers to look like the stem of the flower. Put the other pieces of cucumber at the bottom of the stems to look like leaves. If the cucumber is too big, cut the pieces in half.

6 Put a little tomato catchup on a saucer. Dip a toothpick in the catchup and dot it in the middle of the cheese flowers. Put lots of small dots of catchup in each flower.

12 large square crackers

Boats
2 tablespoons cream cheese
1 cheese slice
2 slices tomato
4 small sticks cucumber
4 tiny triangles cucumber peel

Faces
½ teaspoon tomato catchup
2 tablespoons cream cheese
a few potato sticks
8 raisins
2 radishes

Flowers
2 tablespoons cream cheese
1 tablespoon chopped parsley
1 cheese slice
a little tomato catchup
4 slices cucumber

Makes 12

►·rainbow Sputnik ·◄

½ pound cheese
8 radishes
1 Pepperoni stick
1 celery stick
1 grapefruit

Dip
¼ pound soft cheese with herbs and garlic
4 tablespoons mayonnaise or natural yogurt
1 tablespoon tomato catchup

Serves 6–8

1 Cut the cheese into slices measuring about ¼-inch thick. Cut the slices into cubes, then stick a toothpick into each cube.

2 Cut the radishes in half. Put some of the radishes on the ends of the toothpicks with cheese, put others on toothpicks of their own.

3 Cut the salami stick into 1-inch pieces and put them on toothpicks. Cut the celery stick into 1-inch pieces and pierce each one with a toothpick.

4 Cut a very thin slice off the bottom of the grapefruit so that it sits firmly on a plate. Stick all the toothpicks of food into the grapefruit.

5 In a bowl, mix the soft cheese with the mayonnaise or yogurt and the tomato catchup. When the mixture is smooth, put it in a small dish to serve with the Rainbow Sputnik. Each person takes a toothpick out of the grapefruit and dips it in the cheese mixture.

ꞏ►ꞏ *Cheese Savories* ꞏ◄ꞏ

3 crackers
¼ pound curd cheese
2 teaspoons tomato catchup
2 small bags potato chips (pick your favorite flavor)
a few parsley sprigs

Makes 15

1 Put the crackers in a polythene bag and lay it flat on the work surface. Fold the end of the bag under. Use a rolling pin to crush the crackers. Do this gently, until the crackers are all in crumbs.

2 Put the curd cheese in a bowl. Use a plastic or wooden spoon to stir the cheese. Add the cracker crumbs and stir well until the cheese and crumbs are mixed.

3 Add the catchup and stir until it is evenly mixed with the cheese.

4 Use your fingers to crush the potato chips in their packages. Do this gently so you do not burst the bags. When all the potato chips are broken into little pieces, place them on a large plate.

5 Wash and dry your hands. Take a teaspoonful of the cheese mixture and roll it into a ball. Do this quickly and put the ball on the crushed potato chips. Roll the ball in the potato chips until it is covered all over.

6 Shape all the mixture into balls and place them on a plate. You may put the balls into plain paper candy cases if you like. Gently press a tiny sprig of parsley on top of each ball.

▶· Crunch Munch ·◀

1 orange
1 cup Swiss-style breakfast cereal
4 squares chocolate
a little confectioners' sugar

Makes 12

1 Stand a grater on a board and use the fine side to grate the peel off half the orange. Clean all the peel off the grater. Mix the peel with the cereal in a bowl. Cut the orange in half and squeeze the juice from half, then pour it over the cereal.

2 Break the chocolate into small pieces and place them in a bowl. Put some water in a small saucepan and put it on the stove. Stand the bowl over the pan of water and turn the heat to medium. Stir the chocolate until it has all melted. Take care not to let the water boil up in the saucepan. Turn the heat off. Use pot holders to lift the bowl off the pan.

3 Mix the melted chocolate with the cereal to coat all the little bits. Leave the mixture for a while until the chocolate is beginning to set. While you are waiting, set out 12 large paper candy cases. Use your hands to roll the mixture into balls about the size of a walnut.

4 Put the balls in the paper cases. Put a small spoonful of confectioners' sugar in a small strainer and sprinkle a little sugar on top. Leave to set in a cool place.

▸·Clever Cookies·◂

24 plain sweet cookies
jam or chocolate frosting
½ cup confectioners' sugar
1–2 tablespoons water

Decoration
colored sugar strands
chocolate buttons
a few candied cherries
jellied sweets or
cake decorations

Makes 12

1 Spread 12 cookies with jam or chocolate frosting and press the other cookies on top.

2 Sift the confectioners' sugar into a bowl. Add 1 tablespoon of the water and mix it with the sugar, adding some or all of the remaining water to make a smooth frosting. The frosting must not be too runny.

3 Use a teaspoon to put some frosting in the middle of each Clever Cookie, spreading it out a little to cover the top. Set about 4 of the cookies aside to dry, then sprinkle them with sugar strands.

4 Press a ring of chocolate buttons onto 4 of the cookies while the frosting is wet. Overlap the buttons neatly. Cut 2 candied cherries in half and put half in the middle of the ring of buttons.

5 Put jellied sweets or cake decorations on the other cookies.

6 Leave the frosting to set before putting the cookies on a plate.

ꞏ►ꞏ banana date logs ꞏ◄ꞏ

*1 small banana
1 tablespoon confectioners' sugar
2/3 cup chopped cooking dates
4 tablespoons shredded coconut
1/8 cup crushed plain cookies
4 tablespoons drinking chocolate*

Makes 16

1 Peel the banana and break it into pieces. Put the pieces in a bowl and use a fork to mash them. Stir in the confectioners' sugar and the dates. Mix in the shredded coconut and crushed cookies.

2 Wash and dry your hands. Take small spoonfuls of the mixture and roll them into 16 balls. Flatten the balls and shape them into logs about 1 inch long.

3 Sprinkle the drinking chocolate on a plate. Roll the logs in the drinking chocolate to coat them completely. Put them into paper candy cases and put them in the refrigerator for at least 30 minutes.

▸·jammy birthday cake·◂

1 store-bought plain 8-inch round cake
½ cup jam (your favorite flavor)
scant 2 cups shredded coconut
¼ cup multi-colored candied cherries
angelica

Makes about 10 slices

1 Place the cake on a flat plate. Use a spoon to put the jam on the top of the cake, near the middle. Scrape all the jam off the spoon with a knife.

2 Spread the jam evenly over the top of the cake, taking care that it does not fall down the side. Sprinkle the coconut all over the jam in a nice thick layer.

3 Use a small knife to cut the cherries into quarters. Cut small, thin strips of angelica.

4 Make cherry flowers on the top of the cake. Put pieces of cherry together so they look like petals and use a piece of angelica for a stem.

5 Stick birthday candles in their holders between the cherry flowers. Use a pastry brush to brush any crumbs and bits of coconut off the plate. Tie a bow of ribbon around the side of the cake.

▶· *chocolate* ͦ*range* ƒ*ingers* ·◀

1 store-bought loaf cake (plain or chocolate)
4 tablespoons chocolate frosting
1 tablespoon orange marmalade
white chocolate buttons
candy orange slices

Makes 10

1 Cut the cake into 5 thick slices. Cut each slice in half through the middle to make 10 long bars. Put the bars on a board with the crust side of the cake upward.

2 Put the chocolate frosting in a bowl and gradually beat in the marmalade, adding a spoonful at a time. Spread some of this topping over the cake bars, making small peaks or swirls in it.

3 Press a line of white chocolate buttons on top of some of the bars. Put some candied orange slices on top of the other bars. Arrange the bars on a plate to serve.

·►·*h*idden *C*herries ·◄·

12 candied cherries
½ pound marzipan (see page 10)
a little green food coloring
3 tablespoons superfine sugar

Makes 12

NOTE
Marzipan is a sweet almond paste sold in bars. It is available from large super-markets and delicatessens.

Place a double thickness of paper towels on the counter.

1 Cut the marzipan in half. Set 1 piece aside. Stick a toothpick into the food coloring and dab some on the second piece of marzipan, then knead it evenly until the whole piece is pale green. If it is not green enough, dab more coloring onto it and knead it again.

2 Cut each piece of marzipan into 6 pieces. Take a piece of marzipan and roll it into a ball, then flatten it on the palm of your hand. Put a cherry on the marzipan, then fold it all around the cherry to cover it completely.

3 Roll the marzipan coating into a neat ball. When all the cherries are covered in marzipan, put the sugar on a plate and roll them in it. Put the Hidden Cherries into paper candy cases.

▸·*frosted fruit*·◂

1 lemon
¼ cup superfine sugar

Choose from the following fruit:

red and green eating apples
green and black grapes
cherries with stems
strawberries with stems
mandarin orange segments

Frosted fruit are easy to make. You will need pieces of fruit or small whole fruit.

Wash the fruit. Cut the apples in half and cut out the cores. Thinly slice each piece of apple. Peel the oranges.

Squeeze the juice from the lemon and put it in a small basin.

Push a skewer into a piece of fruit. Dip it into the lemon juice.

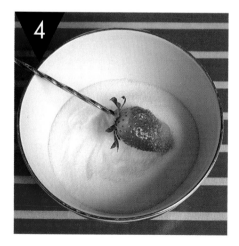

Roll the damp fruit in a bowl of superfine sugar until it is completely coated.

Put the fruit into a paper case. You can use the end of a fork to push it off the skewer.

Candied cherries may also be coated in sugar, but they should not be dipped in lemon juice.

choc-chip ice cream

15-ounce can custard
1 teaspoon vanilla extract
1½-ounce package dessert topping mix
⅔ cup milk
4 ounces chocolate cooking chips

Serves 6

1 Pour the custard into a bowl and stir in the vanilla. Put the dry topping mix into a bowl and slowly stir in the milk. Beat the topping mix until it is thick.

2 Add the topping mix to the custard and use a large metal spoon to fold the two together. Turn the spoon sideways to cut through the mixture, then lift a spoonful of custard over the topping. Do this until the mixture is evenly blended. Lightly stir in the chocolate chips and pour the mixture into a freezer container.

3 Cover the container and put it in the freezer until the mixture is beginning to harden around the edges. This will take about 2 hours, possibly longer. Stir the mixture well to break up all the icy bits, then put it back in the freezer. Leave the ice cream for another 2 hours, or until it is getting hard around the edges. Stir it well as before. Put it back in the freezer and leave for several hours, or overnight, until the ice cream is set.

4 Use a scoop or a spoon to serve the ice cream. If it is very hard, leave the container in the refrigerator for about 30 minutes before trying to scoop the ice cream.

IT'S SIMPLE TO START COOKING

▶· *nutty eggs* ·◀

*4 eggs
¼ cup cottage cheese
2 tablespoons crunchy peanut butter
salt and pepper
4 slices cucumber*

Makes 8

1 Put the eggs in a small saucepan and pour in enough cold water to cover them. Put the saucepan on the stove and turn the heat to high. When the water boils, turn the heat to medium. Boil the eggs for 10 minutes.

2 While the eggs are boiling, put the cottage cheese in a bowl and mash it with a fork until all the lumps are broken. The cheese should be fairly smooth.

3 Turn off the oven. Take care when lifting the saucepan off the stovetop. Put it in the sink and pour off the boiling water. Run cold water onto the eggs and leave them until they are cold.

4 Tap the cold eggs on the countertop to crack their shells, then pull off all the shells. This is easy if you break the very fine skin that lies just underneath the shell. Put the shelled eggs on a plate.

5 Cut the eggs in half lengthwise. Use a teaspoon to scoop out the yolks. Add the yolks to the cottage cheese and mash them with it. Add the peanut butter and mash the mixture together. Stir in a little salt and pepper.

6 Use a teaspoon to put the cottage cheese mixture into the egg whites. Place the stuffed eggs on a plate. Cut the cucumber slices into quarters and stick 2 pieces into the stuffing on each egg.

►·red hot baked potatoes·◄

*2 large potatoes
a little cooking oil
butter*

Serves 4

MICROWAVE TIP
Potatoes cook quickly in the microwave. Put them on a double thickness of paper towels. Prick them in a few places with a fork. Cook them on full power for 12–15 minutes, turning them over halfway through cooking.

1 Set the oven at 400°F. Wash the potatoes, scrubbing them with a small brush. Cut out any bad bits, then dry the potatoes on paper towels. Prick them in a few places and put on a cookie sheet.

2 Brush a little oil all over the potatoes, then bake them for 1–1¼ hours. Use pot holders to remove the cookie sheet from the oven. Hold 1 potato with a clean dishtowel and carefully stick a fork into it. If the potato feels soft in the middle it is cooked. If the middle of the potato still feels hard, then it should be cooked for another 5 minutes before testing it again. Turn off the oven.

3 Hold 1 side of the potato with a dishtowel and cut it in half. Place on individual plates, then top each half with a knob of butter. Cut the other potato in the same way. If you like try some of the following tremendous toppings and fillings.

golden baked potatoes

*2 baked potatoes
¾ cup grated cheese
7-ounce can cream-style corn kernels
salt and pepper*

1 Bake the potatoes and cut them in half following the recipe for Red Hot Baked Potatoes (page 23). Leave the oven on. Have a bowl ready, then use a teaspoon to scoop the soft middle out of the potatoes and put it in a bowl. Take care not to tear the potato skins.

2 Mash the potato. Stir the cheese and the cream-style corn into the potato. Stir in a little salt and pepper.

3 Use the teaspoon to put the potato mixture back into the skins. Place them on a cookie sheet and fork the top of the mixture into short peaks. Bake them for 10–15 minutes, until the top of the filling is lightly browned and slightly crisp.

4 Turn off the oven. Use pot holders to take the potatoes from the oven. Use a clean dishtowel to lift them onto the plates.

potatoes with fishy filling

1 Bake the potatoes and cut them in half following the recipe for Red Hot Baked Potatoes (page 23). Leave the oven on. Turn the sardines and all their sauce into a bowl and mash them with a fork. Use a teaspoon to scoop the middle out of the potatoes, then add it to the sardines and mash it with them. Take care not to tear the potato skins.

*2 baked potatoes
3¾ ounces canned sardines in tomato sauce
2 scallions
salt and pepper
¼ cup grated cheese
1 tomato
4 parsley sprigs*

2

3 Wash and dry the scallions. Cut off any bad bits. Use a pair of scissors to cut the green parts of the scallions in small bits. Save the white ends for a salad. Mix the green scallions with the potato and fish, adding a little salt and pepper.

4 Use a teaspoon to put the potato mixture back into the skins. Place them on the cookie sheet and press the top of the filling down neatly. Sprinkle a little grated cheese on top of each potato. Put back in the oven for 10–15 minutes, until the cheese has melted.

5 Cut the tomato into slices. Turn the oven off. Use pot holders to take the potatoes from the oven and put them on a plate. Top each potato with tomato and parsley.

potatoes with creamy ham topping

*2 baked potatoes
¼ pound cream cheese
⅔ cup diced cooked ham
salt and pepper
8 slices cucumber*

1 Bake the potatoes and cut them in half following the recipe for Red Hot Baked Potatoes (page 23). Turn off the oven.

2 Put the cream cheese in a bowl. Mix the ham with the cream cheese. Mix in a little salt and pepper.

3 Use a teaspoon to pile the cheese and ham on top of the potatoes. Stick 2 cucumber slices into the topping on each potato and serve at once.

beany potatoes

1 Bake the potatoes and cut them in half following the recipe for Red Hot Baked Potatoes (page 23). About 5 minutes before the end of the cooking time for the potatoes, place the baked beans into a small saucepan and put them on the stovetop. Turn the heat to medium. When the beans are bubbling, turn the heat down to the lowest setting.

2 Turn off the oven and stovetop. Use pot holders to take the potatoes from the oven and put them on plates. Top each potato with some of the beans. Sprinkle each one with a little grated cheese if you like.

*2 baked potatoes
8-ounce can baked beans
¼ cup grated cheese (optional)*

OTHER SIMPLE TOPPINGS FOR BAKED POTATOES

★ A spoonful of crunchy peanut butter
★ A spoonful of cottage cheese sprinkled with chopped parsley
★ A spoonful of mayonnaise mixed with a little tomato catchup
★ A hot dog with 6 slices of cucumber and a little mustard
★ Two slices of salami and a sliced tomato
★ A spoonful of flaked tuna fish topped with thick plain yogurt

▸· bean feast ·◂

2 large round crusty bread rolls
½ small onion
2 tablespoons vegetable oil
¼ teaspoon dried sage
8-ounce can baked beans
½ cup grated cheese

Serves 2

1 Use a sharp knife to cut a small cap off the tops of the rolls. Take care not to cut your fingers. Save the slices. Pull the soft middle out of the rolls, leaving just the crisp shells. Be careful not to break the crusts.

2 Put the soft bread on a board and cut it into small pieces. Chop the onion.

3 Put the oil in a small saucepan on the stovetop. Turn the heat to medium. Add the onion to the oil in the pan and cook it, stirring occasionally, for about 5 minutes, or until it is soft but not brown. Stir in the sage and bread. Cook for 5 minutes, stirring all the time.

4 Add the baked beans to the bread mixture and heat them until they are boiling. Stir the beans occasionally. Turn off the oven.

5 Take the pan off the heat and stir in the cheese with a little salt and pepper.

6 Put the bread roll shells on plates and fill them with the bean mixture. Put the roll caps on top and serve at once. A crunchy salad tastes good with these.

▸· toast toppers ·◂

Here are some ideas for hot toast toppings. Make the topping before you toast the bread so the toast does not go cold and hard.
★ *Always take great care when using the broiler. Use pot holders to handle the broiler pan. Before putting food under the broiler have plates ready to put it on when it is cooked. Watch the food all the time it is cooking under the broiler so it doesn't burn.*
★ *All these toppings are for 2 pieces of toast.*

FISH-TOPPED FINGERS
Put ¼ cup cream cheese in a bowl. Add a small jar of salmon paste. Mix the salmon paste with the cheese, then stir in 1 teaspoon tomato catchup. Spread the mixture on the toast and cook it under the broiler until hot. Cut the toast into strips and top each one with a sprig of parsley.

APPLE AND CHEESE
Wash and dry 1 dessert apple. Hold the apple at both ends of the core, then grate it on the coarse side of a grater. Grate all the flesh off until you reach the core. Mix ½ cup grated cheese with the apple. Use a teaspoon to put the mixture all over the toast, then cook.

PEANUT RAREBIT
In a bowl mix 2 tablespoons crunchy peanut butter with 2 tablespoons milk. When the peanut butter is very soft mix in ½ cup grated cheese and add a little salt and pepper. Spread this over the toast. Cook under the broiler until bubbling and lightly browned.

PIZZA TOPPING
In a small bowl, mix 2 tablespoons softened butter or margarine with 1 tablespoon tomato paste and ¼ teaspoon dried marjoram. Mix in a little salt and pepper. Spread the tomato mixture on the toast. Top each slice of toast with a slice of cheese. Cook the cheese under the broiler until bubbling.

Coleslaw Cups

Salads are easy to make and they can taste really scrummy!

small wedge of white cabbage (about 4 ounces)
1 small onion
1 large carrot
1 eating apple
1 tablespoon crunchy peanut butter
6 tablespoons mayonnaise
salt and pepper
4 large lettuce leaves

Serves 4

1 You will need a large board and a sharp knife. Cut any large pieces of core from the cabbage. Cut across the cabbage leaves into thin slices. The slices should fall apart into shreds.

2 Peel and chop the onion. Wash and dry the apple, then cut it into quarters. Cut out the core from each portion of apple. Cut across each apple quarter to make small, thin slices. Trim the ends off the carrot and peel or scrub it, then grate it on the coarse side of a grater.

3 Mix the cabbage, onion, apple and carrot together in a bowl. Put the peanut butter in a small bowl and gradually mix in the mayonnaise. Add a little salt and pepper. Add the peanut mixture to the salad. Use a spoon and fork to mix the dressing into the salad.

4 Wash the lettuce leaves and dry them on paper towels. Put the leaves on a plate and pile the salad onto them.

Sesame Cheese Puffs

¾ cup grated cheese
2 tablespoons sage-and-onion stuffing mix
all-purpose flour for rolling out pastry dough
4 ounces puff pastry dough, thawed if frozen
a little milk or beaten egg
1 tablespoon sesame seeds

Makes 8

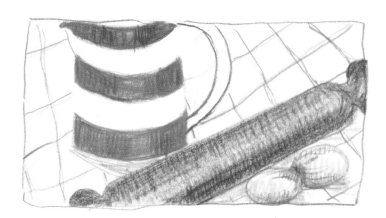

1   In a bowl, mix the cheese with the stuffing mix. Set the oven at 450°F. Have a cookie sheet ready – there is no need to grease it for these pastries.

2   Sprinkle a little flour on a chopping board, then roll out the pastry dough into an 8-inch square. Only roll out the dough away from you and do not press too hard. Press the edges of the dough into shape with your fingers every now and then to make sure it stays square as you roll it.

3   Sprinkle the cheese mixture over half the dough, leaving a narrow border all around the edge. Brush this border with a little water. Fold the other half of the dough over the cheese filling and press it down firmly all over. Press the edges together.

4   Cut the pastry across into 1-inch wide strips. Press each strip together firmly to hold in the filling, then put them on the cookie sheet. Brush the top of each strip carefully with a little milk or egg. Sprinkle a few sesame seeds on top of each strip.

5   Bake the strips for 7–10 minutes. While they are baking, set out a wire rack and put a heatproof mat on the counter. Open the oven to have a look. The pastry strips should be puffed up and golden brown. Turn the oven off. Use pot holders to lift the cookie sheet from the oven. Take great care not to burn yourself.

6   Put the cookie sheet on the mat. Use a spatula or pancake turner to lift the Sesame Cheese Puffs off the cookie sheet and put them on the wire rack to cool.

▶·crunchy ℎot orange·◀

2 chocolate chip cookies
1 orange
½ teaspoon clear honey
2 tablespoons
natural yogurt

Serves 2

Place the cookies on a large piece of plastic wrap and use a rolling pin to crush them. Do not break them too much.

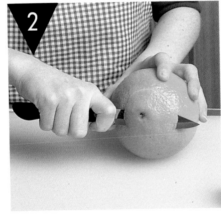

Cut a very small slice of peel off the top and bottom of the orange. Cut the orange in half.

Use a small knife to cut between the orange segments and cut all around the inside of the skin so that the fruit comes out easily.

Place the orange on a tray and spoon on a little honey. Put them under the broiler for 2-3 minutes until they are hot.

Pile the crushed biscuits on top of the oranges.

Decorate each with a spoonful of yogurt.

▶·ɴutty fruit salad·◀

You can use all sorts of fresh fruit in a fruit salad. For a special occasion you may be able to add some of the more expensive exotic fruit. Remember that all pits, cores and seeds must be removed before the fruit is mixed in the salad. If you cannot eat the peel on the fruit, then you must cut that off, too. Try to cut all the pieces of fruit to about the same size.

*2 tablespoons golden raisins
2 oranges
small bunch grapes
a little lemon juice
1 red apple
1 green apple
2 bananas
2 tablespoons clear honey
½ cup chopped nuts
(toasted hazelnuts, mixed nuts or almonds)*

Serves 4

1 Put the golden raisins in a mug. Cut 1 orange in half and squeeze out all the juice from both halves. Pour the juice over the golden raisins and set them aside.

2 Cut a thin slice off the bottom of the other orange. Stand it firmly on the board and cut off all the peel and pith in strips from the top to the bottom of the orange. Take care not to cut off any of the fruit. Cut the orange into slices. Pick out all the pits, then cut each slice into 4 pieces. Put the orange in a salad bowl.

3 Cut all the grapes in half and pick out any pits. Add the grapes to the orange. Put the lemon juice in a small bowl. Cut the apples into quarters. Cut the core from each apple quarter, then cut each quarter into 3 chunks. Dip the chunks of apple in the lemon juice before adding them to the orange.

4 Peel the bananas and cut them into thick slices. Dip the slices in any leftover lemon juice, then add them to the salad. Trickle the honey over the fruit. Pour the golden raisins and orange juice into the salad. Mix the salad without breaking up the fruit. If not serving at once, cover with plastic wrap and place in the refrigerator. Sprinkle the nuts over the top just before serving.

▸·simple biscuits·◂

2 cups all-purpose flour
3 teapoons baking powder
¼ cup margarine
2 tablespoons superfine sugar
⅔ cup milk
extra all-purpose flour
milk for brushing

Makes 12

DIFFERENT SORTS OF BISCUITS

★ Add ⅓ cup raisins with the sugar.
★ Add ½ cup chopped walnuts with the sugar.
★ Do not add the sugar. Instead, add ½ cup grated cheese after you have cut in the margarine to make Cheese Biscuits.
★ Do not add the sugar. Instead, add ½ cup grated cheese and ½ teaspoon Italian seasoning after you have cut in the margarine to make Cheese and Herb Biscuits.
★ Biscuits with cheese added may have a little grated cheese sprinkled on top before baking.

1 Set the oven at 425°F. Grease a cookie sheet. Put the flour in a bowl and stir in the baking powder. Add the margarine. Use a pastry blender to blend the fat with the flour until the mixture resembles fine breadcrumbs.

2 Stir in the sugar. Make a well in the middle of the mixture. Pour the milk into the well and stir the flour into it until you have a soft dough.

3 Turn the dough onto a lightly floured surface. Sprinkle just a little flour on your fingers, then gently knead the dough into a smooth ball.

4 Use a rolling pin sprinkled with a little flour to roll the dough out until it is ¾ inch thick. Use a round cookie cutter measuring about 2 inches across. Dip it in a little flour, then cut out circles of dough. Gather up all the scraps of dough and roll them out to cut out more biscuits.

5 Put the biscuits on the cookie sheet. Brush their tops with a little milk and bake them for 7–10 minutes. While they are cooking put a wire rack ready. Put a heatproof mat on the countertop.

6 Turn off the oven. Use pot holders to take the biscuits from the oven, then use a pancake turner to lift them onto the rack. Eat the biscuits warm, with some butter and jam.

▶ *orange flapjacks* ◀

*1 orange
1/2 cup margarine
4 tablespoons corn syrup
2 tablespoons light brown sugar
1 cup oatmeal*

Makes 16

1 Set the oven at 375°F. Grease an 8-inch square pan really well. Grate the peel from the orange and put it in a small saucepan.

2 Add the margarine and syrup to the orange peel. Put the saucepan on the stove and turn the heat to medium. Stir the mixture in the pan until all the butter has melted. Turn off the heat.

3 Put the oatmeal in a bowl. Pour the melted mixture over the oats and mix them really well. Spoon the mixture into the pan and press it down firmly until the top is smooth and even.

4 Bake the mixture for 30–35 minutes, until it is golden brown and firm. Put a heatproof mat on the countertop. Use pot holders to remove the flapjacks from the oven.

5 Leave the mixture in the pan. When it is just warm, cut it into 16 square pieces. Leave them in the pan until they are cold and firm. Use a spatula to remove the flapjacks.

▶ *brownies* ◀

1 Set the oven at 350°F. Lay a piece of waxed paper on the countertop and stand an 8-inch square baking pan on it. Use a pencil to draw around the bottom of the pan. Cut out the paper along your pencil line. Grease the pan well. Put the square of paper in the bottom of the pan.

2 Put the flour, baking powder, cocoa and sugar in a bowl and mix well. Add the margarine, eggs and vanilla. Stir all the ingredients into a smooth, soft batter. Use a spoon to put the batter into the pan and scrape the bowl clean. Spread the batter out evenly.

3 Bake the Brownies for 40–45 minutes, until risen and the edges have come away from the pan. Put a heatproof mat on the countertop. Use pot holders to remove the pan from the oven. Leave the Brownies in the pan on the mat until cold. Cut into 16 squares.

*3/4 cup all-purpose flour
2 teaspoons baking powder
1/4 cup cocoa powder
1/2 cup soft brown sugar
6 tablespoons margarine
2 eggs
1 teaspoon vanilla extract*

Makes 16

▶·banana muffins·◀

1 cup all-purpose flour
2 teaspoons baking powder
¼ cup sugar
2 tablespoons raisins
1 banana
2 tablespoons margarine
1 egg
6 tablespoons milk

Makes 9

MUFFIN MANIA

You can add other ingredients to Banana Muffins:
★ *Add ½ cup rough chopped walnuts.*
★ *Add 2 tablespoons chopped ready-to-eat dried apricots.*
★ *Add 2 tablespoons peanut butter with the margarine.*

1 Set the oven at 400°F. Grease 9 deep muffin pans or put 9 deep paper cupcake cases in muffin pans. Mix the flour, baking powder, sugar and raisins together in a bowl.

2 Peel the banana, break it into pieces and put them in a bowl. Mash the banana with a fork until it is smooth, then add it to the dry ingredients.

3 Add the margarine and egg. Use a wooden spoon to mix all the ingredients together. Add about half the milk and beat well. Beat in the remaining milk.

4 Use a tablespoon to put the batter into the pans or paper cases, dividing it evenly. Bake the muffins for 20–25 minutes, until they are risen and golden brown. They will rise into peaks and crack slightly.

5 While the muffins are cooking, get out a wire rack and put a heatproof mat on the countertop. Turn off the oven. Use pot holders to remove the muffins. Use a spatula to take the muffins from their pans. Leave them to cool and eat them while they are warm.

REAL MEALS

Menu
Pronto Pasta
Exotic Jelly

ORDER OF WORK

1 Make the Exotic Jelly several hours before the meal or make it the day before.
2 Prepare all the ingredients for the pasta.
3 Cook the pasta and mix it with the ingredients when you are ready to eat.

▶ *pronto pasta* ◀

*1 onion
2 tablespoons vegetable oil
¼ pound mushrooms
½ teaspoon Italian seasoning
14-ounce can choppped tomatoes
salt and pepper
4 hot dogs
12 ounces pasta shapes
½ cup grated cheese
2 tablespoons chopped parsley*

Serves 4

1 Peel and chop the onion. Put the oil in a saucepan over medium heat. Add the onion and cook, stirring occasionally, for about 10 minutes. The onion should be very soft but not browned.

2 While the onion is cooking, cut the end off each mushroom stalk. Rinse the mushrooms under running water, holding the round top up. Rub off any dirt. Slice the mushrooms. Add them to the onion and stir in the Italian seasoning. Add the canned tomatoes and bring the mixture to a boil. Sprinkle a little salt and pepper into the sauce. Turn the heat to the lowest setting. Slice the hot dogs and stir them into the sauce. Continue cooking, uncovered, and stir once in a while.

3 Grate the cheese and set aside.

4 You will need a large saucepan full of water to cook the pasta. Put it on the stovetop. Add a little salt and bring the water to a boil. When the water is boiling add the pasta. Stir the pasta once. Bring the water back to a boil but be ready to turn the heat down so it does not boil over. The pasta should boil without frothing over the edge of the pan. Cook it like this for 15 minutes.

5 Put a colander in the sink. Turn the heat off. Use pot holders to lift the pan of pasta from the stovetop, then pour it into the colander to drain. Put the pasta in a large dish. Turn off the heat under the sauce, then pour it over the pasta. Sprinkle with the cheese and parsley and serve at once. Use a spoon and fork to mix the pasta and sauce together before putting it onto plates.

tropical desserts

2 tablespoons water
3 teaspoons powdered gelatin
2½ cups tropical fruit juice
2 tablespoons shredded coconut
1¼ cups thick plain yogurt
1 tablespoon clear honey
4 orange slices
cookies, to serve

Serves 4

1 Put the water in a bowl and sprinkle the gelatin over it. Do not stir it. Leave the gelatin for 15 minutes. Pour some water into a small saucepan and put it on the stove. Turn the heat to low. Put the bowl over the hot water, then stir the gelatin until it has dissolved completely. It will be clear.

2 Stir the dissolved gelatin into the tropical fruit juice. Divide this mixture between 4 glass bowls and put them in the refrigerator for at least 3 hours until set.

3 Put a piece of foil on the broiler pan and spread the coconut over it. Turn the broiler to a medium setting, then cook the coconut until it is golden. Stir the coconut occasionally with a long-handled wooden spoon so it browns evenly. Turn off the broiler and set the coconut aside to cool.

4 Stir the yogurt with the honey. Swirl the sweetened yogurt all over the set desserts. Sprinkle the coconut over the tops. Cut the orange slices in half and put 2 pieces on each dessert. Serve your favorite cookies with the desserts.

JELLY MAKERS

You can make other set fruit desserts by using different types of fruit juice. Try orange, pineapple or apple. To make a creamy fruit jelly, use fruit-flavored yogurt drink instead of the juice.

HELP POINT
Take great care when handling large saucepans of boiling water. Always make sure there is an adult with you and ask them to lift the saucepan of boiling water to drain the pasta. Always use a pot holder when lifting big hot pans off the stovetop.

CHOPPING PARSLEY

Wash a few sprigs of parsley and break off the stems. Dry the sprigs on a piece of paper towel and put them in a mug. Using the point of a pair of scissors, snip at the parsley in the mug until it is all cut into small pieces. Keep the point of the scissors down in the mug to avoid spilling parsley.

Menu
Pizza
Salad Spectacular
Chocolate Yogurt Swirl

ORDER OF WORK

1 Make the Chocolate Yogurt Swirl in advance and put it in the refrigerator.
2 Collect all the ingredients for the pizza and for the salad. Wash the salad ingredients and set them aside in the refrigerator so they stay crisp.
3 Make the pizza.
4 Make the salad while the pizza is baking.

▶·*pizza*·◀

1 Peel and chop the onion. Cut the green pepper in half. Use a small pointed knife to cut out all the seeds and the core from each half. Cut off all the stem from each half. Cut 1 piece of pepper into long strips, then hold all the strips together and cut across them to make small dice. Repeat with the other half.

2 Put the oil in a small saucepan. Put it on the stove and turn the heat to medium. Add the onion and diced pepper after a few seconds. Cook, stirring, for 5 minutes. Take it off the heat. Stir in the tomato paste, dried marjoram and a little seasoning. Leave to cool.

3 Grease a cookie sheet. Set the oven at 425°F. Put the flour and baking powder in a bowl and add the margarine. Cut the margarine into small pieces. Use a pastry blender to blend the fat into the flour. Mix in the milk to make a dough and press it together with your fingers.

4 Put the dough on a lightly floured surface and knead it lightly into a smooth ball. Put a little flour on a rolling pin, then roll out the dough into a circle about 8 inches across. Put the rolling pin near the middle of the dough, then fold the dough over it. Use the rolling pin to lift the dough onto the cookie sheet. Spread the onion mixture over the dough, leaving a small border all around the edge. Sprinkle the vegetables over the onion. Sprinkle the cheese over the vegetables.

5 Place the ham strips in a criss-cross pattern across the top of the pizza. Bake the pizza for about 15 minutes, until it is risen, bubbling and golden on top. Put a mat on the countertop. Turn off the oven. Use pot holders to take the pizza from the oven. Cut it into wedges to serve.

1 onion
1 green pepper
2 tablespoons vegetable oil
4 tablespoons tomato paste
1 teaspoon dried marjoram
salt and pepper
1 cup all-purpose flour
2 teaspoons baking powder
2 tablespoons margarine
¼ cup milk
extra all-purpose flour
½ cup frozen whole kernel corn,
peas or mixed vegetables
1 cup grated cheese
⅓ cup cooked ham strips

Serves 4

▸·salad spectacular·◂

2 carrots
2 celery stalks
4 scallions
4 tomatoes
1 lettuce heart
1 zucchini
2 tablespoons olive or sunflower oil
1 tablespoon lemon juice

Serves 4

SALAD IDEAS

You can use different vegetables to make this salad. Make sure they are all cut up into small, neat pieces. Try cabbage, cucumber, watercress, mushrooms or cauliflower. Add some crunchy beansprouts, too.

1 Peel the carrots and cut off their ends. Grate them on the coarse side of the grater. Put them on a plate. Wash the celery and use a brush to scrub all the dirt from inside the stalks. Cut across the stalks to make thin slices. Put the celery beside the carrots on the plate, keeping both separate.

2 Wash and trim the ends off the scallions. Peel away any bad bits. Cut the scallions across into small pieces. Push them to one side of the board or put them on a plate. Cut the tomatoes into quarters.

3 Wash and dry the zucchini. Cut off the ends, then cut the zucchini in half lengthwise. Put the cut side of a half down on the board, then cut it into thin slices. Slice the other half in the same way.

4 Wash and dry the lettuce. Use your fingers to tear the leaves into small pieces. You will need a large platter for the salad. Arrange all the vegetables in neat mounds coming from the center of the platter out to the edge. Very carefully trickle the oil all over the salad, then trickle the lemon juice over.

▸·chocolate yogurt swirl·◂

4 squares chocolate
2 tablespoons butter
2 tablespoons corn syrup
4 pots of fruit yogurt or 1 large tub
2 tablespoons chopped nuts

Serves 4

1 Break the chocolate into squares and put them in a heatproof bowl. Add the butter and the syrup. Pour some water into a small saucepan and put it on the stove over medium heat. Stand the bowl in the pan over the water. Heat the mixture until the chocolate melts, stirring occasionally. Make sure that the water does not boil up underneath the bowl. Turn the heat down to low if the water begins to boil.

2 Turn the heat off and use a dishtowel or pot holder to lift the bowl off the water. Set the chocolate mixture aside until it is cool. Pour the yogurt into 4 bowls. Use a spoon to swirl the chocolate mixture through the yogurt. Put the bowls in the refrigerator until you are ready to serve them. Sprinkle the nuts over the top of the yogurt just before serving.

Menu
Tuna Crunch
Rainbow Veg
Marmalade Pears

ORDER OF WORK

1 Prepare the Tuna Crunch, then put it in the oven 20 minutes before you want to eat.
2 Prepare the pears and toss them in lemon juice. Leave them covered in the refrigerator until after you have finished eating the main course.
3 Prepare the vegetables for Rainbow Veg and cook on the stovetop when Tuna Crunch is in the oven.

▶· tuna Crunch ·◀

*1 onion
6½-ounce can tuna in oil
¼ cup all-purpose flour
2 cups milk
salt and pepper
¼ pound mushrooms
¾ cup grated cheese
4 thin slices bread
1 small package potato chips
2 tablespoons butter or margarine
parsley sprigs, to garnish*

Serves 4

1 Set the oven at 375°F. Peel and chop the onion. Open the can of tuna. Holding the lid in place, drain the oil from the can into a small saucepan. Add the onion to the oil and put the pan on the stovetop. Turn the heat to medium and cook the onion, stirring, for about 10 minutes, or until it is soft.

2 Turn the heat to the lowest setting. Add the flour to the onion and stir so that it makes a paste with the oil. Add just a little of the milk and stir it into the paste. Add more milk and stir it in. Continue adding the milk, a little at a time, stirring all the time. Cook the sauce, stirring, until it boils. Turn off the heat. Remove the pan from the heat.

3 Add the tuna from the can. Break the fish into pieces when it is in the sauce. Stir in a little salt and pepper. Rinse the mushrooms under cold water, rubbing off any dirt, then cut them into slices. Add the mushroom slices to the tuna mixture.

4 Add half the cheese to the tuna and stir it in. Turn the tuna mixture into a baking dish.

5 Cut the bread into small cubes and put them in a bowl. Add the remaining cheese. Gently crush the potato chips in their package, taking care not to burst the bag. Tip the potato chips into the bowl and mix them with the bread and cheese. Use a spoon to sprinkle the bread mixture all over the top of the tuna mixture. Put small dots of the butter over the top.

6 Bake the Tuna Crunch for 15–20 minutes, until the cheese has melted and the bread is crisp and brown on top. Use a pot holder to lift the dish from the oven, then put it on a heatproof mat. Garnish the top with sprigs of parsley and serve.

▶· rainbow veg ·◀

*2 carrots
salt and pepper
2 zucchini
½ cup frozen whole-kernel corn or peas
a little butter or margarine*

Serves 4

1 Peel the carrots and cut off their ends. Cut them in half lengthwise. Cut each piece in half again, then across into small dice. Put the carrots in a saucepan and pour in a little water to just cover them. Add a pinch of salt.

2 Wash the zucchinis and cut off their ends. Cut them into thin slices. Put the carrots on the stovetop and turn on the heat to high. When the water is boiling, add the frozen corn or peas. Leave the heat on high until the water boils, then turn it down to medium so it is just bubbling, or simmering.

3 Cook the carrots and corn for 10 minutes. Add the zucchini to the other vegetables and cook for just 2 minutes. The zucchini should be hot but not soggy. Put a colander in the sink. Turn off the heat, then drain the vegetables in the colander. Put them in a serving dish and dot with some butter or margarine, adding a sprinkling of pepper.

▶· marmalade pears ·◀

*4 firm pears
2 tablespoons lemon juice
1 orange
4 tablespoons orange marmalade
cream, plain yogurt or ice cream, to serve*

Serves 4

1 Remove the stems from the pears and peel them thinly. Cut them into quarters, then cut the core out of each piece of pear. Cut the quarters into chunks and place them in a bowl. Spoon the lemon juice over and mix it into the pears. The lemon juice will stop the pears from turning brown. Cover the bowl and put the pears in the refrigerator until you are ready to serve them.

2 Grate the peel from the orange on the fine side of the grater. Put the peel in a small saucepan. Add the marmalade. Set a strainer over the saucepan. Cut the orange in half and squeeze the juice from both halves through the sieve. Put the saucepan on the stovetop. Turn on the heat to low and stir the mixture until the marmalade has melted. Turn off the heat.

3 Put the pears into individual bowls and spoon some of the marmalade sauce over each portion. Spoon a little cream, plain yogurt or ice cream on top and serve at once.

HELP POINT
When making a sauce, it is easier to ask an adult to pour in the milk slowly while you stir the paste all the time.

Menu
Pork 'n' Potato Loaf
Stir-fry Vegetables
Banana Splits

ORDER OF WORK

1 Make the jam sauce for the Banana Splits.
2 Make the Pork 'n' Potato Loaf.
3 Prepare the vegetables while the Pork 'n' Potato Loaf is cooking.
4 Stir-fry the vegetables as soon as the Pork 'n' Potato Loaf is removed from the oven.
5 Make the Banana Splits just before you are ready to eat them.

·▶·pork 'n' potato loaf·◀·

1 You will need a 7½- × 3½-inch bread pan and a piece of waxed paper. Stand the tin on the paper and draw all around it with a pencil. Cut out the shape following your pencil line. Grease the pan and put the paper in it. Set the oven at 375°F.

2 Put the meat in a bowl. Peel the onion, then grate it on the coarse side of the grater. Take care not to grate your fingers. It is difficult to grate the last little piece, so cut that up very small. Add the onion to the meat. Mix in the sage with plenty of salt and pepper. Break one egg into a cup, then tip it into the bowl and mix it really well with the meat.

3 Peel the potatoes. Wash and dry them. Grate them on the coarse side of the grater. Squeeze the grated potato, then put it in another bowl. Break the second egg into a cup, then tip it into the potato. Add the flour and plenty of salt and pepper. Mix well.

4 Put half the potato mixture into the pan and press it down with the back of a spoon. Put all the meat mixture on top, pressing it down so that it is smooth. Put the remaining potato mixture into the pan and spread it out evenly. Bake the loaf for 1¼ hours, until it is brown and crisp on top.

5 Have a heatproof mat ready for the pan. Use pot holders to remove the pan from the oven. Turn off the oven. Put a plate upside down on the pan. Use the pot holders to hold them, then turn the pan upside down onto the plate. Lift the pan off. Peel the paper off.

6 Cut the tomato into slices and arrange them on top of the loaf. Add some parsley sprigs.

1 pound ground pork
1 onion
1 teaspoon dried sage
salt and pepper
2 small eggs
1 pound potatoes
4 tablespoons all-purpose flour
1 tomato
a few parsley sprigs

Serves 4

▶ Stir-fry Vegetables ◀

1 leek
4 celery stalks
1 red pepper
½ pound green cabbage
3 tablespoons vegetable oil
salt and pepper

Serves 4

HELP POINT
Turning hot food out onto a serving plate is difficult so always ask an adult to help.

▶ banana splits ◀

⅜ cup jam
3 tablespoons orange juice
4 small bananas
8 small scoops vanilla ice cream
8–12 strawberries (optional)

Serves 4

1 Trim the ends off the leek. Cut in half lengthwise, then wash both pieces under cold running water to get rid of all the grit. Drain off the water, then cut both pieces into thin slices.

2 Wash the celery, scrubbing off all the dirt. Cut the stalks into thin slices. Cut the pepper in half. Cut out the stem and the core with all the seeds. Rinse both halves under running water. Cut the pieces in half lengthwise, then across into short thin strips.

3 Cut any large pieces of core from the cabbage. Cut across the leaves to give fine slices that fall into shreds as they are cut. Put the cabbage in a colander and wash it under cold water. Leave to drain.

4 Put the oil in a large skillet or wok. Put it on the stove-top and turn the heat to high. Add the leeks, celery and red pepper. Stir the vegetables all the time and cook them for 3 minutes.

5 Add the cabbage and sprinkle in a little salt and pepper. Continue stirring the vegetables. Reduce the heat to medium and cook for another 5 minutes, stirring all the time. Turn off the heat and serve at once.

STIR-FRY SPECIALS

Lots of different vegetables may be stir-fried. Try sliced onion, small baby corn ears, cut green beans, bean-sprouts, small pieces of cauliflower, sliced Brussels sprouts, sliced scallions or mushrooms.

1 Put the jam in a bowl. Pour some water into a small saucepan and put it on the stovetop. Stand the bowl over the water and turn the heat to medium. Stir the jam until it has melted. Turn off the heat and use pot holders to lift the bowl off the saucepan.

2 Stir the orange juice into the jam, then leave it until cold. Peel the bananas and cut them in half lengthwise. Put the 2 halves slightly apart on plates or dishes.

3 Put 2 scoops of ice cream between each pair of banana halves. Use a teaspoon to trickle the jam sauce over the top. Add 2 or 3 strawberries to each Banana Split if you like and serve at once.

Menu
Rainbow Rice
Doughnut Dessert

ORDER OF WORK

1 Prepare the fruit for the dessert.
2 Make the Rainbow Rice.
3 Finish the Doughnut Desserts while the Rice is cooking and put them in the refrigerator or in a cool place.

·rainbow rice·

1   Peel the onion and cut it in half. Cut both halves into thin slices. Peel the carrot and cut off its ends. Cut it in half lengthwise, then across into slices. Scrub the celery under running water. Cut the stalks across into slices.

2   Cut the bacon slices across into thin strips. Pour the oil into a saucepan and put it on the stovetop. Turn the heat to medium. Add the bacon to the pan and cook, stirring, until it is just beginning to brown.

3   Add the onion, carrot and celery. Stir and cook for 5 minutes. Add the rice and marjoram, stir well and cook for 2–3 minutes.

4   Pour the stock into the pan. Do this very carefully as it will cause a lot of steam. So make sure your arm is not stretched over the pan. Add a little salt and pepper. Stir and bring it to the boil. Turn the heat down and cover the pan. Cook for 10 minutes.

5   Add the peas. Stir once and put the lid on the pan. Cook for another 15–20 minutes, until the rice has absorbed all the stock. While it is cooking, roughly chop the peanuts. Divide between 4 plates or bowls and sprinkle the peanuts and Parmesan on top. Serve at once.

*1 onion
1 carrot
2 celery stalks
¹⁄₂ pound bacon
2 tablespoons vegetable oil
1 cup long-grain brown rice
¹⁄₂ teaspoon dried marjoram
2 cups chicken stock
salt and pepper
1¹⁄₃ cups frozen peas
¹⁄₂ cup salted peanuts
grated Parmesan cheese, to serve*

Serves 4

CHICKEN STOCK

Stocks add flavor to cooked dishes. Chicken stock is made by boiling the bones from roast chicken with an onion, a carrot, a celery stalk and some parsley. The water must cover all the ingredients and it is cooked for at least 1 hour or up to 3 hours. The liquid is strained and when it cools it may be frozen. Instead of making stock with bones, you can buy stock cubes that are dissolved in boiling water.

▶ *doughnut dessert* ◀

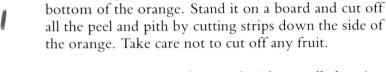

¼ *pound raspberries*
1 orange
3 tablespoons confectioners' sugar
4 ring doughnuts

Serves 4

1 Put the raspberries in a bowl. Cut a fine slice off the bottom of the orange. Stand it on a board and cut off all the peel and pith by cutting strips down the side of the orange. Take care not to cut off any fruit.

2 Cut the orange into slices and pick out all the pits. Cut the slices into small pieces. Mix them with the raspberries. Sprinkle 2 tablespoons of the confectioners' sugar over the fruit and set aside for at least 30 minutes.

3 Put the doughnuts on individual plates. Fill the hole in the middle of the doughnuts with the raspberries and orange. Spoon any fruit juices over the tops.

4 Just before serving the dessert, put the remaining confectioners' sugar in small strainer. Sprinkle just a little over the top of the fruit in each doughnut.

FRUITY FILLINGS

Instead of the raspberries and orange, make a fruit salad (page 30) to fill the doughnuts. You can also fill the doughnuts with canned pineapple or with canned fruit pie filling.

HOW TO SPROUT BEANS

You will need some small, green mung beans and a large jam jar. Take about enough beans to fill the jar a quarter and put them in a strainer. Wash the beans under cold water, put them in the jar and pour in water to cover them. Leave them to soak overnight.

Next day, drain off the water and rinse the beans. Put them back into the rinsed jar. Cover the jar with a piece of paper towel and put a rubber band around it. Remove the paper and rinse and drain the beans every day. In about 3 days they will have started to grow shoots. After 4–5 days the shoots will be long enough to eat. Do not let them grow too long or they will taste bitter.

Menu
Fish Stick Quiche
Baked Beans
Rice Cocktails

ORDER OF WORK

1 Make the Rice Cocktails and put them in the refrigerator.
2 Make the Fish Stick Quiche.
3 Heat the baked beans 5 minutes before the end of the cooking time for the quiche.

▎►· *fish stick quiche* ·◄▎

*1½ cups all-purpose flour
6 tablespoons margarine
1–2 tablespoons cold water
4 scallions
2 eggs
⅔ cup milk
salt and pepper
¾ cup grated cheese
6 frozen fish sticks
parsley sprig*

Serves 6

1 Set the oven at 375°F. Put the flour in a bowl. Add the margarine and cut it into small pieces. Use a pastry blender to blend the fat into the flour. Add 1 tablespoon cold water and mix the pastry with a knife. If it does not form large lumps add the rest of the water. Press the pastry together into a ball.

2 Get out an 8-inch quiche dish. Put a little flour on your rolling pin. Roll out the dough on a lightly floured surface into a circle large enough to line the quiche dish. To measure the dough, hold the dish over it. There should be enough all around the edge to come up the side of the dish.

3 Put the rolling pin on the dough. Fold the dough over the pin, then use the rolling pin to lift it into the quiche dish. Press the dough down into the dish. If you have any breaks in the dough just press them together with your fingers. Roll the rolling pin over the top of the dish to cut off the extra dough.

4 Prick the dough all over with a fork. Put a sheet of waxed paper in the dish. Sprinkle some dried peas over the paper. Bake the dough for 10 minutes. Put a heatproof mat on the countertop. Use pot holders to lift the dish from the oven. Lift the peas and paper out of the pastry case. Lower oven temperature to 350°F.

5 Cut any bad bits off the scallions, then wash them and cut them across into small pieces. Beat the eggs with the milk, adding a little salt and pepper.

Sprinkle the cheese all over the bottom of the quiche. Scatter the scallions over the cheese, then pour in the eggs and milk. Arrange the fish sticks in the quiche like the spokes of a wheel. Bake the quiche for 50–60 minutes, or until the top of the fish sticks are brown and crisp and the egg is set.

Have a heatproof mat ready to put the quiche on. Use pot holders to lift the dish from the oven. Turn off the oven. Place a sprig of parsley in the middle of the quiche and serve cut wedges. This can be served hot or at room temperature.

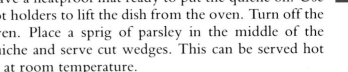

baked beans

16-ounce can baked beans

Serves 4

1 Get out a small saucepan. Open the can of beans and pour them into the pan. Put the pan on the stovetop and turn the heat to medium.

2 Stir the beans occasionally until they are just boiling and heated through. Turn off the heat. Serve with the Fish Stick Quiche.

BEANS ON TOAST

To make Beans on Toast, toast 4 slices of bread while the beans are heating. Spread some butter or margarine on the toast, then put the slices on plates. Spoon the beans over the toast and serve at once.

rice cocktails

¼ cup candied cherries
2 tablespoons raisins
11-ounce can mandarin oranges
small piece angelica
17-ounce can creamed rice pudding

Serves 4

1 Cut the cherries into quarters and put them in a small bowl with the raisins. Open the can of mandarin oranges. Hold the lid in place and drain all the juice from the can into another bowl. Add 2 tablespoons of the juice to the cherries and raisins. The rest of the juice may be used to make a drink.

2 Leave the cherries and raisins to soak for 30 minutes. Cut the angelica into small pieces. Open the rice pudding and put it in a bowl.

3 Add the mandarin oranges and angelica to the rice. Pour in the cherries and raisins and stir well. Divide the Rice Cocktails between 4 glass bowls. Put in the refrigerator for at least 30 minutes.

Menu
Sandwich Supper
Tomato Salad
Coconut Cookie Cake

ORDER OF WORK

1 Make the Coconut Cookie Cake in advance and put it in the refrigerator.
2 Make the Sandwich Supper and leave it to soak for 30 minutes before cooking.
3 Make the Tomato Salad while the Sandwich Supper is cooking.

▸·*Sandwich Supper*·◂

*8 slices bread
6 tablespoons butter
1 tablespoon wholegrain mustard
4 thick slices cheese
extra butter for greasing the dish
3 eggs
1¼ cups milk
salt and pepper*

Serves 4

1 Cut the crusts off the bread. Spread the slices with the butter. Spread 4 slices with mustard and lay the cheese on top. Press the remaining bread slices on top to make cheese sandwiches.

2 Grease a large baking dish. Cut the sandwiches across into 4 triangular pieces. Put these small sandwiches in the dish, overlapping them to fit them all in.

3 Crack the eggs 1 by 1 into a cup, putting them into a bowl when you are sure there are no bits of shell in each. Use a whisk to beat the eggs. Gradually pour in the milk and whisk again.

4 Add a little salt and pepper to the egg mixture. Then pour it slowly all over the sandwiches. Leave to soak for 30 minutes so the bread has time to absorb the egg and milk.

5 Set the oven at 350°F. Bake the sandwiches for 40–50 minutes, until they are golden brown on top and all the egg is set.

6 Put a heatproof mat ready on the countertop. Use pot holders to remove the dish from the oven. Turn off the oven. Serve the Sandwich Supper freshly cooked but take care when eating it – the cheese is very hot!

OTHER SANDWICH FILLINGS TO TRY

★ Ham
★ Cream cheese and scallion
★ Cheese and peanut butter

▶·tomato Salad·◀

8 tomatoes
2 scallions
salt and pepper
1 tablespoon vegetable oil
½ teaspoon vinegar

Serves 4

1 Cut the tomatoes in half. Cut out the core and stem end from each half. Cut the halves into thin wedges.

2 Place the tomato wedges on a plate. Trim any bad bits from the scallions, then wash and dry them. Cut them across into small pieces, then sprinkle them over the tomatoes.

3 Sprinkle a little salt and pepper over the tomatoes. Trickle the oil all over the salad. Sprinkle the vinegar over and serve.

▶·Coconut Cookie Cake·◀

16 coconut cookies
2 tablespoons orange juice
1¼ cups whipping cream
1 chocolate Flake
6 candied cherries
12 angelica leaves

Serves 6

Sprinkle orange juice over the cookies until they are moist, but not soggy.

Whip the cream in a bowl until it stands in soft peaks. Spread a little cream on 3 cookies, press them into a stack and add another on the end.

HOW TO MAKE ANGELICA LEAVES

Cut some angelica into thin strips. Cut across the strips at an angle to make diamond shapes. Turn these on end to represent leaves.

Line the cookies up and put plastic wrap completely around them. Chill the cookie cake for at least 1 hour, turn the cookie cake on its side on a plate. Then cover it with the remaining cream, crumble the Flake over the top and add cherries with angelica leaves.

Menu
Pastacular
No-cook Chocolate Fudge Tart

ORDER OF WORK

1 Make the Chocolate Fudge Tart several hours before the meal so it has time to set.
2 Prepare all the ingredients for the pasta dish at least 1 hour before you intend to serve the meal.

▶·*p*astacular·◀

1 Trim the ends off the mushroom stalks. Rinse the mushrooms, wiping off any bits of dirt. Dry them on paper towels, then slice them.

2 Cut the sausage into fairly thin slices. Peel and chop the onion.

3 Three-quarters fill a large saucepan with water and put it on the stovetop. Add a little salt and turn the heat to high. When the water boils add the pasta and give it a stir. Stand by to turn the heat down to medium as soon as the water boils. If you leave the heat on high the water will boil over. Boil the pasta for 15 minutes. Put a colander in the sink. Turn the heat off and pour the pasta into the colander. Leave to drain.

4 Put the butter in a medium saucepan and put it on the stovetop. Turn the heat to medium. Add the onion to the butter and cook, stirring, for 5 minutes.

5 Add the flour to the onion and stir to make a paste. Slowly pour the milk into the pan, stirring all the time. Stir in the frozen beans. Keep stirring until the sauce boils and thickens. Once it has boiled, cook the sauce for 3 minutes.

6 Add the mushrooms to the sauce and stir in the cheese. Sprinkle a little salt and pepper into the sauce. Cook stirring, until the cheese has melted. Taste the sauce to check whether it has enough seasoning.

7 Add the cooked pasta to the sauce, stir well and cook gently for about 5 minutes, until it is hot. The beans should be hot and lightly cooked, with a bit of crunch.

8 Heat the broiler. Turn the pasta mixture into a flame-proof serving dish and put it under the broiler until golden brown on top. Use pot holders to remove the dish from under the broiler. Turn the heat off.

¼ pound mushrooms
¾ pound smoked sausage
1 onion
8-ounces pasta spirals
2 tablespoons butter
6 tablespoons all-purpose flour
2½ cups milk
salt and pepper
1 cup frozen cut green beans
½ cup grated cheese

Serves 4

▸·no-cook chocolate fudge tart·◂

4 ounces vanilla wafers
4 tablespoons butter

Filling
6 squares semi-sweet chocolate
4 tablespoons butter
6 tablespoons corn syrup
1 tablespoon cocoa powder
4 cups plain cake crumbs
¼ pound cream cheese
2 tablespoons confectioners' sugar
2 tablespoons orange juice

Serves 4–6

1 Put the cookies in a plastic bag. Twist the end closed, then fold it over. Use a rolling pin to crush the cookies, taking care not to break the bag.

2 Put the butter in a medium saucepan. Put the pan on the stovetop and turn the heat to medium. When the butter has melted, turn the heat off and tip all the cookies into the butter. Stir well.

3 Turn the buttered cookies into a 6-inch quiche dish. Press them all over the bottom and up the sides of the dish in a thin, even coating. Put the dish in the refrigerator to chill the cookie mixture.

4 Put the cake in a bowl. Wash and dry your hands. Crumble the cake into small, even pieces.

5 Break the chocolate into squares and put it in a saucepan. Add the butter, syrup and cocoa. Put the pan on the stovetop and turn the heat to low. Stir the mixture until the butter has melted and the corn syrup is runny. Turn off the heat.

6 Put the cake crumbs in a bowl. Pour the chocolate mixture over the cake crumbs and mix really well. Carry on mixing until every bit of cake has absorbed the chocolate. Put the chocolate cake mixture into the cookie case and press it down evenly.

7 Put the cream cheese in a bowl with the confectioners' sugar and the orange juice. Beat well until the cheese is very soft. Pile this on top of the tart and swirl it out evenly.

8 Chill the tart for at least 1 hour before serving it cut into wedges.

FAST FOODS

·hot dog kabobs·

2 hot dogs
4 small tomatoes
8 button mushrooms
a little oil
salt and pepper

Mustard Sauce
1 tablespoon French mustard
4 tablespoons plain yogurt or fromage frais
1 scallion

1 Cut each hot dog into 4 pieces. Cut the tomatoes in half. Thread 4 pieces of hot dog, 4 mushrooms and 4 tomato halves on a long metal skewer. Thread the rest of the ingredients on another metal skewer.

2 Mix the mustard with the yogurt or fromage frais. Trim the ends off the scallion. Wash and dry it on paper towels, then cut it into small pieces. Stir the scallion into the sauce.

3 Heat the broiler. Brush a little oil over the kabobs and sprinkle with a little salt and pepper. Put the kabobs under the grill for 3 minutes. Use pot holders to hold the end of the skewers and turn the kabobs over. Cook for another 3 minutes.

4 Serve the mustard sauce with the kabobs.

SERVING IDEAS

★ Have pita bread with the kabobs. Warm the pita at the bottom of the broiler while you cook the kabobs. Split the bread down one side and fill it with the food off the skewers.
★ Arrange the kabobs on a plate of shredded lettuce.
★ Serve Coleslaw Cups (page 27) with the kabobs.
★ Heat a small can of baked beans or spaghetti in tomato sauce to go with the kabobs.

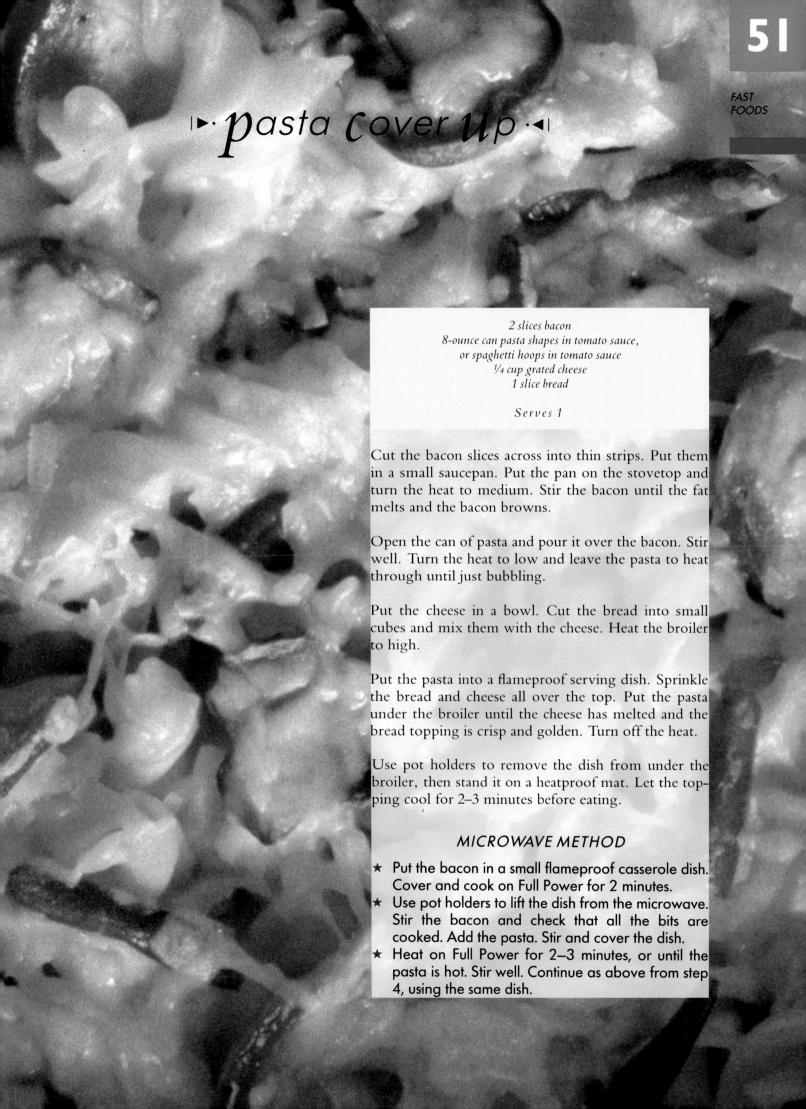

▶ pasta cover up ◀

2 slices bacon
8-ounce can pasta shapes in tomato sauce,
or spaghetti hoops in tomato sauce
¼ cup grated cheese
1 slice bread

Serves 1

Cut the bacon slices across into thin strips. Put them in a small saucepan. Put the pan on the stovetop and turn the heat to medium. Stir the bacon until the fat melts and the bacon browns.

Open the can of pasta and pour it over the bacon. Stir well. Turn the heat to low and leave the pasta to heat through until just bubbling.

Put the cheese in a bowl. Cut the bread into small cubes and mix them with the cheese. Heat the broiler to high.

Put the pasta into a flameproof serving dish. Sprinkle the bread and cheese all over the top. Put the pasta under the broiler until the cheese has melted and the bread topping is crisp and golden. Turn off the heat.

Use pot holders to remove the dish from under the broiler, then stand it on a heatproof mat. Let the topping cool for 2–3 minutes before eating.

MICROWAVE METHOD

★ Put the bacon in a small flameproof casserole dish. Cover and cook on Full Power for 2 minutes.
★ Use pot holders to lift the dish from the microwave. Stir the bacon and check that all the bits are cooked. Add the pasta. Stir and cover the dish.
★ Heat on Full Power for 2–3 minutes, or until the pasta is hot. Stir well. Continue as above from step 4, using the same dish.

⊷·burger salad·⊷

1 eating apple
1 small carrot
1 scallion
salt and pepper
1 oval-shaped bread roll
2 lettuce leaves
1 frozen hamburger
4 slices cucumber

Serves 1

MICROWAVE METHOD

★ *Check the weight of the hamburger. Put it on a plate.*
★ *Cook on Full Power. Allow 1½–2 minutes for a 2-ounce hamburger. A 4-ounce hamburger takes 3–3½ minutes.*

1 Peel the apple. Grate all the flesh off the core on the coarse side of the grater. Put the grated apple in a bowl.

2 Peel the carrot and trim off the ends. Grate it on the coarse side of the grater. Mix the grated carrot with the apple. Trim any bad bits off the scallion. Wash and dry it. Cut it across into small pieces. Mix the scallion with the salad, adding a little salt and pepper.

3 Split the roll lengthwise without cutting it right through. Wash and dry the lettuce leaves. Put them in the roll. Put the salad in the roll. Heat the broiler.

4 Cook the hamburger under the broiler for 3–5 minutes. It should be well browned. Use a pancake turner and a fork to turn the hamburger over. Cook the second side for 3–5 minutes. Turn the heat off.

5 Cut the hamburger across the middle in half. Put these onto the salad in the roll. Add the cucumber slices.

▸·barbecue-style vegi burger·◂

½ small onion
1 clove garlic
1 tablespoon vegetable oil
2 teaspoons demerara sugar
½ teaspoon French mustard
2 tablespoons tomato catchup
2 tablespoons water
8-ounce can baked beans in tomato sauce
1 frozen vegetable burger

Serves 1

MICROWAVE METHOD

★ Mix the onion, garlic and oil in a bowl. Cover and cook on Full Power for 3 minutes.
★ Stir in the other sauce ingredients and the beans. Cover and cook on Full Power for 2–3 minutes, until the beans are hot.
★ Put the vegetable burger on a plate. Cook on Full Power for 2–3 minutes, until it is heated through.

1 Chop the onion. Peel the garlic clove, then cut it into small pieces. Mix the onion and garlic in a small saucepan with the oil.

2 Put the pan on the stove and turn the heat to medium. Cook, stirring occasionally, for about 8 minutes, until the onion is soft. Stir in the sugar, mustard, catchup and water. Heat, stirring, until the mixture bubbles.

3 Add the baked beans to the barbecue sauce and stir well. Leave over low heat until the beans are hot and bubbling. Heat the broiler.

4 Cook the vegetable burger under the broiler for 3–5 minutes, until browned. Use a pancake turner and fork to turn the burger over. Cook for 3–5 minutes until the second side is browned. Turn off the broiler.

5 Put the vegetable burger on a plate. Turn off the oven. Spoon some of the barbecue beans over the vegetable burger and put the remainder on the plate beside it.

▸· chicken noodles ·◂

1 onion
1 green pepper
¼ pound mushrooms
1 cup diced skinless cooked chicken or ham
8-ounce block Chinese egg noodles
2 tablespoons vegetable oil
2 tablespoons soy sauce
1 cup frozen mixed vegetables

Serves 2

MICROWAVE METHOD

★ Soak the noodles as described above.
★ Put the onion and pepper in a dish with the oil. Cover and cook on Full Power for 3 minutes.
★ Add all the remaining ingredients except the noodles. Mix well. Cover and cook on Full Power for 7–10 minutes. Stir once during cooking.
★ Add the noodles. Mix well and serve.

1 Peel and chop the onion. Cut the green pepper in half. Cut out the stalk, core and remove all the seeds. Cut each piece of pepper in half lengthwise, then across into short, thin strips.

2 Trim the ends off the mushroom stalks. Rinse the mushrooms under running water and wipe off any dirt. Slice the mushrooms.

3 Put the noodles in a bowl. Pour boiling water over the noodles to cover them. Leave to stand for 5 minutes. Use pot holders and pour the noodles into a colander in the sink and leave to drain.

4 Pour the oil into a large skillet or wok and put it on the stovetop. Turn the heat to medium. Add the onion and green pepper. Cook, stirring, for 5 minutes. Add the mushrooms and chicken. Cook, stirring all the time, for 5 minutes.

5 Pour in the soy sauce and add the frozen mixed vegetables. Stir well. Cook for 7–10 minutes, stirring occasionally, until the vegetables are hot.

6 Add the noodles to the pan. Mix all the ingredients together and cook for 2 minutes to heat the noodles. Turn the heat off. Divide the noodles between 2 bowls or plates.

▸·*h*ash-tash·◂

*½ pound potatoes
2 tablespoons all-purpose flour
salt and pepper
12-ounce can corned beef
7-ounce can whole kernel corn
1 egg
2 tablespoons vegetable oil
2 tablespoons butter or margarine*

Serves 4

Peel the potatoes, wash them, then grate them on the coarse side of the grater. Squeeze all the water from the grated potato. Put it in a bowl. **1**

Add the flour and plenty of salt and pepper. Mix the flour into the potato. Add the corned beef. Use a knife to cut up the corned beef. Mix the beef and potatoes together using a spoon. The corned beef is soft enough to break up as you mix. **2**

Drain the corn, then stir it and the egg into the mixture. Put a skillet on the stove and spoon in the oil. Turn the heat to high for 30 seconds, until the oil is hot. Turn the heat down to medium. **3**

Add all the potato mixture to the pan and spread it out evenly. Press it down firmly all over. Put a lid or large heatproof plate on top of the pan. Cook for 15–20 minutes, until the potatoes are cooked. **4**

Heat the broiler to medium. Use pot holders to remove the lid. Turn off the stove. Dot the butter or margarine over the top of the hash, then put the pan under the broiler. Cook until the top of the hash is golden and crisp. Have a heatproof mat ready to put the pan on. Turn off the broiler. **5**

Cut the hash into wedges and use a pancake turner or spatula to lift them out of the pan. **6**

*C*hicken-corn
▸· *C*howder ·◂

*2 scallions
small knob of butter or margarine
½ cup diced cooked chicken
8½-ounce can cream-style corn
4 tablespoons milk
salt and pepper
a few packet croûtons*

Serves 1

Cut any bad bits off the scallions. Cut them across into small pieces. Put a small knob of butter or margarine in a small saucepan. Put the pan on the stovetop and turn the heat to low.

When the butter has melted, add the scallions. Stir, then leave to cook very gently for 5 minutes.

Add the chicken to the scallions. Stir in the cream-style corn. Pour in the milk and stir to mix. Add a little salt and pepper. Increase the heat to medium and heat the soup until it is just bubbling. Cook for 2 minutes, stirring.

Turn the heat off and pour the soup into a bowl. Sprinkle packet croûtons over the top.

Salami Stick roll-ups

1 Cut the crusts off the bread. Spread a thin layer of cheese over both slices. Spread a little tomato catchup over the soft cheese.

2 Cut the salami stick in half. Put 1 piece across the end of each slice of bread. Roll up carefully without squeezing out the cheese and catchup. Wrap a piece of plastic wrap around each sandwich and leave for 5 minutes.

3 Peel the carrot and cut the ends off. Cut in half lengthwise. Cut each half lengthwise into 2 sticks. Scrub the celery stalks and cut them across in half.

4 Unwrap the roll-ups and put them on a plate with the celery and carrot sticks. Eat roll-ups and vegetable sticks together.

*2 thin slices bread
a little low-fat cream cheese
a little tomato catchup
1 Pepperoni stick
1 small carrot
1 celery stalk*

Makes 2

▶ tuna rarebit rolls ◀

1 Spread the tuna mixture thickly over the half-toasted rolls. Put them back under the broiler until the topping is brown. Turn off the broiler.

2 Put the rolls on plates and top each half with cucumber slices and a sprig of parsley. Take care when eating – the topping is very hot!

3 Drain the liquid from the tuna. Put the tuna in a bowl. Mix the cheese with the tuna. Add the milk. Sprinkle in some salt and pepper.

4 Mix the ingredients really well so they combine to make a thick paste.

5 Heat the broiler. Slice the rolls in half through the middle. Put the rolls on the rack with the cut sides down. Cook until the tops are golden. Turn the rolls over. Cook until they are only lightly browned.

4½-ounce can tuna
½ cup grated cheese
2 tablespoons milk
salt and pepper
2 round bread rolls
about 8 cucumber slices
4 parsley sprigs

Serves 2

▶ toasted sandwich ◀

1 Heat the broiler. Spread a little butter or margarine on the bread slices. Sandwich the bread and the cheese together, pressing them down firmly, with the un-buttered sides of the bread on the outside.

2 Put the sandwich under the broiler until it is golden brown on one side. Turn the sandwich over and toast the second side. Turn off the broiler and eat the sandwich while it is hot. Take care when you bite the filling – the cheese gets very hot!

TREMENDOUS TOASTED SANDWICHES

Try these fillings.
★ Cheese, thinly sliced apples and a little chopped onion.
★ Mashed canned sardines with sliced pickled cucumber.
★ Mashed tuna fish with cottage cheese.
★ A thin slice of corned beef and a spoonful of baked beans.
★ A slice of cooked turkey with 2 teaspoons of cranberry sauce.
★ A slice of cooked pork with 2 teaspoons applesauce.
★ A cooked bacon slice with a sliced tomato.
★ Peanut butter with sliced hot dogs.

SANDWICH TOASTERS

If you have a special electric sandwich toaster ask an adult to show you how to use it. The toaster should be heated up before the sandwiches are put in it, then they are cooked for about 3 minutes. They will be very hot.

▸· taco tomato scramble ·◂

*a few lettuce leaves
4–6 cucumber slices
1 egg
1 tablespoon milk
salt and pepper
1 tomato
a little butter or margarine
1 taco shell
parsley sprig (optional)*

Serves 1

1 Wash and dry the lettuce leaves. Tear them into small pieces and put them on a plate with the cucumber. Crack the egg into a bowl. Add the milk with a little salt and pepper. Use a whisk to beat the egg and milk together.

2 Cut the tomato in half. Place the flat side down on the board, then cut both halves across into slices. Holding the slices in place cut across them to make small pieces of tomato.

3 Have a heatproof mat ready on the countertop. Put a small knob of butter or margarine in a small saucepan. A non-stick pan is best. Put it on the stovetop and turn the heat to medium. When the butter melts, pour the egg into the pan. Stir it all the time over the heat until it begins to get thick and set.

4 As soon as the egg is set and creamy, remove the pan from the stovetop. Put the pan on the mat and turn off the heat. Add the tomato to the egg and stir lightly. Put the taco shell on the plate with the salad. Spoon the egg mixture into it. Add a sprig of parsley if you like. Eat at once.

·►· tostada toppers ·◄·

1 avocado
1 lettuce heart
16 slices cucumber
4 tomatoes
4 thin slices cooked ham
4 packet tostadas
¾ cup grated cheese

Makes 4

MICROWAVE METHOD

Place 2 tostadas on a plate and cook on Full Power for about 2 minutes, until the cheese has melted. Cook the other tostadas separately. Take care — the topping is extra hot when cooked in the microwave!

MORE TOPPERS

★ Salami, sliced tomato and sliced mozzarella cheese
★ Sliced hot dogs, corn relish and cheese
★ Mashed avocado topped with rind-less bacon rashers
★ Mashed canned sardines with onion slices and cheese

1

Cut all around the avocado. Hold both sides firmly and twist one half, then pull it off the pit. Ask an adult to help you to remove the pit. If the pit is loose it will come out easily. If not, stick the point of a knife into it and pull it out. Take great care not to stick the knife into your hand.

2

Cut both pieces of avocado in half lengthwise. Peel the skin off each piece and cut the flesh into 3 slices. When you have sliced all the avocado put it on a plate and cover it with plastic wrap.

3

Wash and dry the lettuce. Break the leaves into small pieces using your fingers. Divide the lettuce between 4 plates and put 4 cucumber slices on top of each portion. Cut the tomatoes into slices.

4

Heat the broiler. Put the tostadas on the broiler pan and put a slice of ham on top of each. Sprinkle the cheese all over the ham.

5

Put the tostadas under the broiler until the cheese has melted and lightly browned. Turn off the broiler. Use a pancake turner to lift the tostadas and put 1 on each plate, on top of the lettuce and cucumber or beside it. Divide the tomato and avocado slices between the tostadas. Serve at once.

▶·bacon and salad croissant·◀

1 croissant
4 slices cucumber
1 small tomato
1 lettuce leaf
1 slice bacon

Makes 1

1 Slice the croissant in half through the middle. Arrange the cucumber slices overlapping on the bottom half of the croissant then put it on a plate.

2 Cut the tomato into slices and put them on top of the cucumber. Wash and dry the lettuce. Break the leaf into 2 or 3 pieces, then put them on top of the tomato.

3 Put the bacon in a small pan and put it on the stove-top. Turn the heat to medium and cook until the fat runs from the bacon and the underneath is brown. Use a fork to turn the bacon over. Cook the second side until it is browned. Turn off the heat.

4 Place the slice of bacon on top of the salad. Put the top back on the croissant. Eat at once, while the bacon is still hot and the salad is crunchy.

▶·*Sausage and apple filler*·◀

1 large oval-shaped bread roll
2 tablespoons cream cheese
pinch dried sage
1 lettuce leaf
½ eating apple
1 scallion
1 pork link sausage

Makes 1

1 Slice the roll in half through the middle. Spread both halves with a little cream cheese. Sprinkle with the sage.

2 Wash and dry the lettuce leaf. Cut the core out of the apple and cut it into slices. Trim any bad bits off the scallion, wash and dry it. Cut the scallion into 3 pieces.

3 Put the lettuce leaf on the bottom half of the roll. Arrange the apple and scallion on top.

4 Heat the broiler. Cook the sausage until it is golden brown all over. Turn it 2 or 3 times during cooking. Have a small plate with a piece of paper towel on it ready.

5 Turn off the heat. Put the sausage on the paper. Pat the fat off the sausage, then cut it at an angle into thin slices. Put these on top of the apple and scallion. Put the top on the roll and eat at once.

·►·quick Soup Special·◄·

2 slices bacon
½ small onion
10¾-ounce tomato soup
1 tablespoon snipped chives

Serves 1

1 Cut the bacon across into thin strips. Put them in a small saucepan. Wash the spring onion and dry it. Cut the onion into thin slices and add them to the pan.

2 Put the pan on the stovetop and turn the heat to medium. Cook, stirring often, until the fat runs from the bacon. Continue to cook for 5 minutes, or until the onion is softened.

3 Open the can of soup and pour it into the pan. Stir and heat gently until the soup is just boiling. Turn off the heat.

4 Pour the soup into a bowl and sprinkle with the chives. Eat at once – but remember it is very hot!

MICROWAVE METHOD

Put the bacon and onion in a dish. Cover and cook on Full Power for 4 minutes. Stir the mixture twice during cooking. The bacon must be cooked. Add the soup and heat, without a cover on the dish, on Full Power for 2 minutes. Stir the soup halfway through cooking and again before you pour it into a bowl.

THROWING A PARTY

PACK UP A PICNIC

When the weather is fine, invite a few of your friends to go on a picnic. If you are asking more than your Mum and Dad can take in their car, ask your friends' parents to come along, too.

Write out invitations on pieces of colored paper.

Picnic Party

*Please come to my picnic on
Saturday August 10th at The Park.
We will be at the parking lot at 2 pm.
Please bring something to sit on.
Love
Jamie*

Make sure that all the parents know about the picnic and where to meet.

WHAT TO TAKE

★ A plastic sheet to put on the ground
★ Blankets to sit on
★ Plenty of paper napkins or paper towels
★ A paper tablecloth
★ Paper or plastic plates and mugs
★ 1 or 2 huge plastic bags to put all your garbage in.

WHAT TO PLAN

★ Food – take food that is easy to pack and to eat. Try the Picnic Menu or make your favorite goodies.
★ Games – plan 2 or 3 games that everyone can play together outside. Pack anything you need to play.
★ Prizes – pack a prize for each game. Ask an adult for help with this one.
★ Fun pack – plan a small fun pack for each of your guests. For example, include a balloon with a piece of string and a whistle or a toy that unrolls and squeaks when you blow it. Add a small pack of Iced Diamond Cookies or a fruity bar is a good idea.

DO NOT

★ Let anyone wander off. Everyone has to stay together and join in the games.
★ Leave any litter. Make clearing up a fun activity at the end of the party. Give a little prize for the person who collects the most garbage.

Picnic Menu
Mini Meatballs
Pizza Sticks
Cheese Savories (page 13)
Sandwich Rolls
Mini Quiches
Orange Flapjacks (page 32)
Brownies (page 32)

▶·*mini Meatballs*·◀

1 onion
1 pound sausage meat
2 tablespoons crunchy peanut butter
2 cups fresh bread crumbs
1 small egg
salt and pepper
1 teaspoon dried sage

Makes about 30

Peel the onion and grate it on the coarse side of the grater. Cut up the last bit very small.

Put the onion in a bowl with the sausagemeat, peanut butter and breadcrumbs. Break an egg into a cup and tip it into the bowl.

Mix the ingredients together. Break the sausagemeat up with the edge of a spoon, then pound all the other ingredients into it by pressing with the back of a spoon.

Wet your hands and roll a lump of mixture into a ball about the size of a walnut.

Put these balls in a large skillet on the stovetop and turn the heat to medium. When the meatballs begin to sizzle, move them around the skillet as they cook until they are brown all over. Put them on a double thickness of paper towels on a plate to cool.

▶ Sandwich rolls ◀

*3 eggs
2 tablespoons mayonnaise
½ cup grated cheese
salt and pepper
12 large, thin slices bread*

Makes 24

Put the eggs in a small saucepan and pour in enough cold water to cover them. Put the pan on the stovetop and turn the heat to high. As soon as the water boils, turn the heat down to medium. Boil the eggs for 10 minutes. Turn off the heat. Pour off most of the boiling water down the sink. Run cold water over the eggs in the pan, then leave them to cool.

Crack the eggs and peel off the shells. Put them in a bowl and mash them with a fork until they are very fine. Stir in the mayonnaise. Mix the cheese into the eggs with some salt and pepper.

Cut the crusts off the bread. Spread a slice with some of the egg mixture. Roll it up from the short side, pressing it firmly together without squeezing out the filling. If the bread will not stay rolled, put 2 toothpicks through it. Cut the roll in half.

Make all the other rolls, then pack them close together in a container or in plastic wrap. The toothpicks may be removed when the sandwiches are packed.

▶ pizza sticks ◀

*1 cup all-purpose flour
4 tablespoons margarine
½ teaspoon dried marjoram
½ cup grated cheese
salt and pepper
1 teaspoon tomato paste
1 tablespoon water
extra all-purpose flour
beaten egg or milk, to glaze*

Makes 12

Put the flour in a bowl. Add the margarine, then use a knife to cut the margarine into small pieces. Use a pastry blender to blend the fat with the flour.

1

Add the marjoram and the cheese. Stir in some salt and pepper. In a mug or small bowl, mix the tomato paste with the water, than add the mixture to the dry ingredients. Use a spatula or a blunt knife to mix the ingredients together. When the mixture forms large lumps, use your fingers to press it together into a ball.

2

Set the oven at 400°F. Grease a cookie sheet. Sprinkle a little flour on the work surface, then gently knead the dough until smooth. Flatten it into a big sausage, then cut this into 12 equal pieces. Roll the pieces of dough into thin sticks measuring about 6 inches long.

3

Put the dough sticks on the greased cookie sheet, leaving a little room between them. Brush them with a little beaten egg or milk. Bake for 15–20 minutes, until the sticks are golden brown.

4

While the sticks are baking, set out a wire rack to put them on. Put a heatproof mat on the countertop. Turn off the oven. Use pot holders to take the cookie sheet from the oven. Use a spatula or pancake turner to lift the Pizza Sticks off the cookie sheet and put them on the wire rack to cool.

5

▶·*m*ini *q*uiches·◀

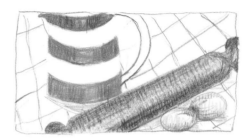

1   Set the oven at 375°F. Have ready 15 tartlet tins. Put the flour in a bowl. Add the margarine and cut it into small pieces. Use a pastry blender to rub the fat into the flour.

2   Add the cold water to the dough, then use a blunt knife to mix it together. If the dough does not form clumps add just a few more drops of water. Press the dough into a ball.

3   Place the dough on a lightly floured surface and flour the rolling pin. Roll out the dough thinly. Use a 2½–3-inch cookie cutter to cut out circles of dough. Dip the cutter in flour so it does not stick to the dough. Put a circle of dough in each tin, pressing it in neatly.

4   Make the filling. Put the cream cheese in a bowl. Trim the bad bits off the scallions, wash and dry them. Cut them across into small pieces, then mix them with the cheese.

5   Stir in the eggs. Add the grated cheese to the filling with a little salt and pepper. Stir well. Use a teaspoon to put this filling into the quiches. Place the tins on a cookie sheet.

6   Bake the quiches for 20–25 minutes. They should be brown and set on top. Have a heatproof mat or board ready to put the cookie sheet on. Use pot holders to remove the cookie sheet. Turn off the oven. Leave the quiches in the tins for 10 minutes. Have ready a wire rack. Then use a spatula to help lift them from the tins and put them on a wire rack to cool.

2 cups all-purpose flour
½ cup margarine
about 2 tablespoons cold water

Filling
½ pound cream cheese
4 scallions
2 eggs
½ cup grated cheese
salt and pepper

Makes 15

▶· vegetable dippers ·◀

These are easy to make. Use some or all of the following vegetables.

*celery stalks
carrots
cauliflower flowerets
radishes
cucumbers
red or green peppers
scallions*

1 Scrub celery stalks under cold running water. Trim the ends, then cut the stalks into 2–inch pieces.

2 Peel carrots and cut off their ends. Cut them in half lengthwise. Cut each piece in half lengthwise, then across to make neat sticks.

3 Cut the thick core off cauliflower. Separate the head into small flowerets. Wash and dry them.

4 Trim the tops of radishes and wash them. Dry on paper towels.

5 Peel cucumber and cut it into 2-inch pieces. Stand each piece up and cut down into quarters.

6 Cut peppers in half. Cut out the stems, core and all the seeds. Cut the peppers across into ½-inch wide slices.

7 Trim any bad bits off scallions. Cut off the green part (save it for a salad or put it in the dip), leaving 2 inches of the white part.

▶· cottage cheese dip ·◀

*1 cup cottage cheese
4 tablespoons mayonnaise
4 tablespoons snipped chives
1 tablespoon tomato paste
salt and pepper*

Serves 6

1 Put a strainer over a bowl. Place the cottage cheese into the strainer. Use a wooden spoon to rub all the cheese through the strainer. Scrape the cheese off the underneath of the strainer when you have finished.

2 Add the mayonnaise, chives and tomato paste. Mix well, then sprinkle in a little salt and pepper. Stir to mix in the seasoning. Cover with plastic wrap and chill the dip for 30 minutes.

SNIPPED CHIVES

3 Chives are long, thin and green – they look a bit like grass. They taste like onions. They should be washed, then dried on paper towels and snipped. All this is much easier if you hold the bunch of chives together neatly. Holding the bunch firmly at one end, use a pair of scissors to snip the chives into tiny bits. Gradually move your fingers back so you can cut up the whole bunch.

COOKIE HUNT

This is a good idea for an indoor or out-door party. Simply invite your friends to come over for a cookie hunt.

*We are having a cookie hunt on
Wednesday April 6th
at 75 Holly Close
Please come at 4 pm.
Love
Sarah*

Cut out circles of paper to look like cookies and write your invitations on them. If you like, draw a circle in the middle to look like frosting and add a cherry. Or, draw light brown cookies with dark dots for chocolate chips.

WHAT TO PLAN

★ Make lots of different cookies.
★ Wrap the cookies in plastic wrap then wrap them in colored paper.
★ Just before the party, hide the cookies all over the house. In summer you can have a cookie hunt in the garden.
★ Give prizes for the child who finds the most cookies.
★ Have a prize for the child who finds the largest cookie.
★ Have a prize for the child who finds the best decorated cookie.
★ Have a booby prize for anyone who does not find a single cookie.

COOKIE HATS

If you like, ask everyone to come wearing a cookie hat. These can be made from cardboard and tied on with string. They should have different decorations on top. Some hats could look like sandwich cookies, others like chocolate chip cookies or frosted cookies. Give a prize for the best cookie hat.

Cookie Hunt Menu
Pizza Sticks (page 65)
Vegetable Dippers (page 67)
Cottage Cheese Dip (page 67)
Lots of different cookies
Chocolate Milk Shakes

▸·*basic cookies*·◂

2 cups all-purpose flour
½ teaspoon baking powder
½ cup butter or margarine
⅓ cup confectioners' sugar
2 egg yolks
1 teaspoon vanilla extract

Makes 30–35

1 Set the oven at 350°F. Grease 2 cookie sheets. Put the flour and baking powder in a bowl. Add the butter or margarine and cut it into small pieces. Use a pastry blender to rub the fat into the flour.

2 Stir in the confectioners' sugar. Make a well in the middle of the mixture. Add the egg yolk and vanilla extract. Stir the egg and vanilla into the mixture until it forms clumps. Then use your fingers to press the mixture together into a dough.

3 Cut the dough in half. Put a little flour on a board and on your rolling pin. Knead the piece of dough into a smooth flat round, then roll it out to about ¼ inch thick. Use cookie cutters to cut out the cookies.

4 Cut the cookies in all sorts of different shapes. Re-roll all the trimmings. Repeat with the second portion of dough.

5 Put the cookies on the cookie sheets. Bake for about 15 minutes, until lightly browned.

6 Use pot holders to take the cookie sheets from the oven. Turn off the heat. Use a spatula to lift the cookies off the sheets. Put them on the wire rack to cool. Add toppings and decorations to the cold cookies.

TOPPINGS

★ Melted chocolate with chopped nuts.
★ Glacé frosting. Follow the directions for making the frosting used on Clever Cookies (page 15). Top the cookies with halved cherries or chocolate chips.
★ Melt 2 tablespoons crunchy peanut butter with 4 squares chocolate.
★ Orange frosting – mix 1 cup confectioners' sugar with 1–2 tablespoons orange juice.

DIFFERENT FLAVOURED BISCUITS

Chocolate – add 2 tablespoons cocoa powder with the icing sugar.
St Clement's – add the grated rind of 1 lemon and 1 orange with the icing sugar.
Walnut – add 50 g/2 oz finely chopped walnuts with the icing sugar.
Chocolate Chip – stick chocolate polka dots into the cookies before baking them.

DECORATIONS

★ Colored sugar strands or chocolate strands
★ Chocolate buttons, milk and white
★ Small candies
★ Silver balls
★ Yellow candy balls
★ Halved or quartered candied cherries with strips of angelica
★ Slivered almonds

▶·peanut cookies·◀

6 tablespoons margarine
⅓ cup soft light brown sugar
1 teaspoon vanilla extract
1 cup all-purpose flour
1 teaspoon baking powder
¾ cup salted peanuts

Makes about 15

1 Set the oven at 350°F. Grease 2 cookie sheets. Put the margarine in a bowl with the sugar. Beat well until the mixture is very soft and light.

2 Stir in the vanilla extract. Add all the flour, baking powder and the peanuts. Mix well until all the ingredients are combined. This will make a soft dough.

3 Take small lumps of the dough and roll them into balls about the size of walnuts. Place the balls well apart on the cookie sheets. Flatten the balls with a fork. Bake for about 15 minutes, until golden.

4 Put out a wire rack. Use pot holders to remove the cookie sheets from the oven. Have a heatproof mat ready. Turn off the oven. Leave the cookies on the sheets for 2 minutes, then use a spatula to put them on the wire rack. Leave until cold.

►·*p*inwheel *C*ookies·◄

1 quantity Basic Cookies (page 69)
2 tablespoons cocoa powder

Makes about 32

1 Set the oven at 350°F. Grease 2 cookie sheets. Make up the cookie dough. Cut it in half. Put a little flour on a board. Knead 1 piece of dough and flatten it into a smooth flat round. Put 1 tablespoon cocoa in the middle. Fold the dough around the cocoa. Knead the dough until all the cocoa is mixed in. Mix in the rest of the cocoa in the same way.

2 Lightly flour the board and the rolling pin. Roll out the chocolate dough to an oblong measuring 10 × 8 inches. Set this aside. Knead the plain dough into a smooth flat round, then roll it out to the same size.

3 Put the rolling pin on the chocolate dough and roll the dough over it. Lift the dough on top of the plain dough. Lightly press the two layers of dough together.

4 Roll up the dough from the long end like a jelly roll. Press it together firmly. Use a sharp knife to cut the roll into ¼-inch slices. Put these on the cookie sheet. Bake for 15–20 minutes. Put out a wire rack.

5 Use pot holders to take the pinwheels from the oven. Have a heatproof mat ready. Use a spatula to lift the pinwheels from the cookie sheets. Put them on the rack to cool.

►·*C*hocolate *m*ilk *s*hakes·◄

2 tablespoons cocoa powder
3 tablespoons boiling water
about 1 tablespoon sugar
2½ cups cold milk
4 chocolate candy sticks

Makes 4

1 Put the cocoa in a large heatproof pitcher. Carefully mix in the boiling water. Stir in the sugar. Beating all the time, slowly pour in the milk. Beat until the milk is frothy.

2 Pour the shakes into 4 small glasses and put a chocolate candy stick in each.

ROLLER PARTY

Invite your friends to a roller disco, then take them home for something to eat. If you prefer you could organize a skateboarding party, a swimming party, a trip to the theater or to the movies. Take advantage of whatever is going on in the area.

WHAT TO PLAN

★ Where to go – check out facilities at youth centers and sports centers. Ask for details about reduced prices for parties. See what is on at the theater or movies. Make sure your parents are involved in your plans.
★ Invite everyone to meet at your house before going on to the entertainment. Your parents should plan the transportation.

PARTY PLANNING

★ Have a bright paper tablecloth with matching paper napkins
★ Have plastic or paper plates
★ Decorate the room with paper streamers and balloons
★ If you want to play music, choose the records.

Menu
Nutty Eggs
(page 22)
Sesame Cheese
Puffs (page 28)
Stuffed
Tomatoes
Savory Rolls
Coleslaw Cups
(page 27)
Garlic Bread
Lemon Jelly
Cheesecake

▶ Savory rolls ◀

1 onion
25 g/1 oz butter or margarine
100 g/4 oz fresh breadcrumbs
100 g/4 oz chopped mix nuts
3 tablespoons chopped parsley
1 teaspoon dried mixed herbs
50 g/2 oz cheese
1 egg
225 g/8 oz puff pastry dough (thawed if frozen)
beaten egg, to glaze

Makes 18

1 Set the oven at 220°C/425°F/gas 7. Grease 2 baking trays. Peel and chop the onion. Put the butter or margarine in a small saucepan. Put the pan on the hob and turn the heat to medium. When the fat has melted add the onion. Cook, stirring occasionally, for 5 minutes. Turn off the heat.

2 Put the breadcrumbs, onion, nuts, parsley and dried herbs in a bowl. Add the grated cheese to the mixture. Add the egg with a little salt and pepper. Mix well to combine all the ingredients.

3 Sprinkle a little flour on the work surface and on your rolling pin. Roll out the pastry dough into an oblong measuring 30 × 45 cm/12 × 18 in. Cut this in half lengthwise. Divide the breadcrumb mixture in half. Use a teaspoon to put half all down the middle of 1 strip of pastry. Put the rest down the second strip of pastry. Brush the edges of the pastry with a little water and fold them over to completely cover the filling.

4 Press the pastry edges together firmly. Cut the rolls into 5 cm/2 in lengths. Press the filling in at the ends. Put the rolls on the baking trays with the join in the pastry underneath. Brush a beaten egg over the top. Bake for 10–15 minutes, until the pastry is puffed and golden. Set out a wire rack and heatproof mat. Use oven gloves to put the rolls on the rack to cool.

·stuffed tomatoes·

2 eggs
6 medium tomatoes
1 cup fresh bread crumbs
2 tablespoons snipped chives
2 tablespoons chopped parsley
parsley sprigs, to garnish

Makes 6

Boil your eggs (see Nutty Eggs on page 22) and shell when they are cool. Put them in a small bowl and mash them well.

Cut a thin slice off the top and chop into small pieces. Scoop out the soft middle, putting it all in a bowl.

Drain the tomatoes upside down on paper towels. Add the bread crumbs, chives and parsley to the bowl.

Mix well, sprinkling in some salt and pepper.

Mix in the mashed egg with the tomato and bread crumb mixture.

Use a teaspoon. Arrange the stuffed tomatoes on a plate. Garnish with parsley sprigs.

ꞏ▸ꞏ *garlic bread* ꞏ◂ꞏ

*¼ cup butter
1 small clove garlic
1 tablespoon chopped parsley
1 8-inch French stick*

Makes 10 pieces

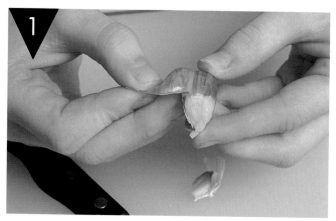

Set the oven at 400 F. Put the butter in a small basin and soften it by creaming it with the back of a wooden spoon. Peel the garlic and put the clove in a garlic crusher.

Crush the garlic into the butter, scraping all the bits off the crusher. Add the parsley and mix well.

Cut the loaf into 10 slices. Lay a piece of foil, large enough to wrap the loaf, on the countertop. Spread the butter thinly on the slices and press them all back together on the piece of foil. Fold the foil around the loaf, pinching the edges together to seal the packet.

Put the bread in the oven for 10-15 minutes, until all the butter has melted and the bread is hot and crisp. Have a basket ready and put some absorbent paper towels or a napkin in it. Use pot holders to remove the bread from the oven. Turn the heat off. Put the bread in the basket and serve at once.

·►· lemon jelly cheesecake ·◄·

Put the cookies in a plastic bag. Twist the end of the bag closed but do not seal it. Use a rolling pin to crush the cookies in the bag. Do this fairly gently so you do not break the bag.

1

Put the butter in a medium saucepan. Put the pan on the stove and turn the heat to medium. When the butter has melted, turn off the heat. Add the cookies to the butter and stir. Turn the cookies into a 9-inch quiche dish. Scrape all the bits from the saucepan. Press the cookies evenly over the bottom of the dish. Put the dish in the refrigerator.

2

Prepare the lemon gelatin dessert according to the directions on the package. Put in the refrigerator until it is just beginning to set. It should be rather like syrup.

3

Put the cream cheese in a bowl. Add a little of the lemon mixture and beat well. Gradually beat in all the lemon gelatin. Turn this mixture into the quiche dish. Spread it evenly over the cookie base. Put the cheese-cake in the refrigerator until it is set.

4

Turn the cream into a bowl and use a whisk to whip it until it is thick enough to stand up in soft peaks. Put a star piping tip in a pastry bag. Put the tip and the bag in a measuring cup, folding the ends of the bag over the outside of the cup. Spoon the cream into the bag, scraping every little bit out of the bowl.

5

Gather up the ends of the pastry bag. Hold the tip near the edge of the cheesecake and squeeze out some cream. At the same time gently move the bag around to pipe a swirl. Pipe swirls all around the edge of the cheesecake. Put chocolate buttons between the swirls. Cut the cheesecake into wedges to serve.

6

4 ounces vanilla wafers
¼ cup butter
3-ounce package lemon-flavored gelatin dessert
1 pound cream cheese
⅔ cup heavy cream
chocolate buttons, to decorate

Serves 12

AFTERNOON TEA PARTY

Making a special party for the rest of the family, or for 1 or 2 friends, can be fun. Make a special cake and some sandwiches. Turn store-bought ice cream into a real treat with a chocolate sauce. To make the table look special, add a pozy of flowers and tie pretty ribbon bows around some paper napkins.

TABLE POZY

Find a small vase or a small jar. Cut small flowers to make a table decoration. If you want to tie a bow of ribbon around the jar it is best to do this first. If you use narrow ribbon you can tie several small bows and leave the ends of the ribbon to trail prettily. Use a pitcher to pour some water into the vase, then add the flowers.

DECORATIVE NAPKINS

Wrap a piece of ribbon loosely around each paper napkin, then tie it in a bow. If you like, put a small flower in the bow just before the party begins.

SETTING THE TABLE

Put a tablecloth on the table and put your flowers in the center. Put out a knife and plate for each person. Arrange the napkins on the plates. Set cups and saucers (if you need them) separately on a tray so the tea can be poured easily.

Afternoon Tea Party Menu
Sandwich Rolls (page 65)
One-stage Carrot Cake
Peach Melba
Iced Tea

▶·*One-stage Carrot Cake*·◀

1 cup grated carrots
½ cup margarine
½ cup superfine sugar
1½ cups all-purpose flour
3 teaspoons baking powder
1 teaspoon ground cinnamon
2 eggs
⅓ cup raisins
1 cup walnut pieces
1 orange

Cream Cheese Frosting
8 ounces cream cheese
2 tablespoons confectioners' sugar
2 tablespoons orange juice
a few walnut halves, to decorate

Makes a 7-inch cake

DECORATION IDEA
You can make some marzipan carrots to decorate the cake. Make them the day before you are going to decorate the cake. Color about 4 ounces marzipan with a little orange food coloring. Knead the color into the marzipan until it is evenly mixed. Cut the marzipan into 6 pieces. Roll each piece into a short sausage, then mold them into carrots, with a point at one end and a thick part at the other end. Pat the thick end of the marzipan flat. Stick a few thin pieces of angelica into the flat end of each carrot. Very gently mark lines across the carrots.

1 Take a piece of waxed paper and stand a 7-inch deep round cake pan on it. Draw around the bottom of the pan. Cut out the circle of paper. Grease the pan and put the paper in the bottom of it. Set the oven at 325°F.

2 It is important to grate the carrots before you weigh them. Cut off their ends and peel them, then grate the carrots on the medium-fine side of the grater. Put the weighed carrots in a bowl.

3 Add the margarine, sugar, flour, baking powder and cinnamon. Break 1 egg into a cup, then tip it into the bowl. Break the second egg and tip it in. Add the raisins and walnuts. Now mix all the ingredients together until they are thoroughly combined. The mixture should be soft and creamy.

4 Grate the rind off the orange. Stir it into the cake batter, then turn the batter into the pan. Use a rubber spatula to scrape all the batter from the bowl. Spread the mixture evenly in the pan. Bake the cake for 1½ hours.

5 The cake is cooked when it is risen and golden brown. To test if the middle is cooked, stick a clean, metal skewer into the cake. Take the skewer out again. If there is any sticky batter on the skewer the cake is not cooked in the middle.

6 Set out a wire rack. Use pot holders to lift the cake from the oven. Turn it out onto the rack to cool.

7 To make the Cream Cheese Frosting, put the cream cheese in a bowl. Add the confectioners' sugar and orange juice. Beat well until the cheese is soft and smooth.

8 Put a doily on a plate and put the cake on it. Spread the frosting thickly on top of the cake. Use a spatula to make large swirls in the frosting. Decorate the cake with walnut halves. Tie a large bow of ribbon around the side of the cake.

▶· peach melba ·◀

½ pound raspberries
4 tablespoons confectioners' sugar
15½-ounce can peach slices
8 scoops store-bought vanilla ice cream

Serves 4

1 Place a strainer over a bowl. Put the raspberries in the strainer and use a spoon to press them through. Scrape the raspberry purée from underneath the strainer when you have finished.

2 Stir the confectioners' sugar into the raspberry purée.

3 Open the can of peaches and drain off the liquid. Divide the peach slices between 4 glass bowls. When you are ready to serve the Peach Melbas, put 2 scoops of ice cream into each bowl. Spoon the raspberry sauce over the tops. Serve at once.

▶· iced tea ·◀

2 Earl Grey tea bags
3¾ cups boiling water
4 lemon slices
4 sprigs of mint
4 ice cubes

Serves 4

1 Put the tea bags in a heatproof pitcher or in a teapot. The water must be freshly boiling in the kettle. Pour it into a measuring cup, then pour it straight onto the tea bags. Take great care when using the kettle and pouring boiling water. Ask an adult to stand near by.

2 Leave the tea for 7 minutes. Use a spoon to lift out the tea bags. If the tea is in a pot there is no need to lift out the bags but the tea should be poured into a heatproof pitcher. Cover the pitcher with plastic wrap and leave the tea until cold. Put the tea in the refrigerator for at least 30 minutes.

3 Pour the tea into 4 glasses. Add an ice cube to each. Float a slice of lemon on the tea and add a sprig of mint to each glass. Offer a bowl of sugar with the tea.

THE BRUNCH BUNCH

Be a trend-setter and invite your friends to a brunch party. Plan to go out after you have eaten your brunch or organize party games and stay at home. Brunch is ideal if you want to go out to the movies afterwards or if you want to go for a walk.

Brunch combines both breakfast and lunch at about 11.30 am. Remember to put the time on the invitation and let your friends know what you have planned for afterward.

Tim invites you to brunch
on Saturday June 6th
at 44 Georgie Villas.
Afterward we shall be going to see the new
Space Thrill movie.
Please come at 11.30 am.
Love
Tim

WHAT TO PLAN

★ If you want to go to the movies or to any other form of entertainment make sure you allow enough time for eating and for getting there.
★ Make sure that walks or transportation are organized by the adults.
★ If you are planning a walk, make sure all your guests come with suitable clothes and shoes.

Brunch Menu
Grapefruit Cocktails
Bacon Kabobs with bread rolls
Banana Muffins (page 33)
Yogurt Fizz

▶· yogurt fizz ·◀

2½ cups plain yogurt
carbonated orange drink
4 orange slices

Serves 4

1 Spoon the yogurt into 4 glasses. Add a little carbonated orange and stir. Top up with more carbonated orange.

2 Cut a slit into the center of each orange slice. Slip the slices over the rim of the glasses and put drinking straws into each Yogurt Fizz. Serve at once.

▶· grapefruit Cocktails ·◀

2 large grapefruit
2 large oranges
about 4 teaspoons clear honey
4 mint sprigs

Makes 4

1 Cut a slice off each fruit. Stand a grapefruit on a board and cut off strips of peel down the side until all the peel and pith are removed. Repeat with all the fruit.

2 When the fruit is peeled, cut it into slices. Pick out the pits and cut the slices into chunks. Put these in a bowl and mix well. Cover and chill for at least 1 hour.

3 Divide the fruit between 4 small glass bowls and trickle about 1 teaspoon of honey over each. Top with a mint sprig. Stand the glass bowls on saucers. Put a teaspoon on each saucer.

▶· bacon kabobs ·◀

4 slices bacon
4 link sausages
4 small tomatoes
8 button mushrooms
a little vegetable oil
4 oval-shaped bread rolls
a little butter or margarine
watercress sprigs, to garnish

Serves 4

Cut the bacon slices in half. Roll up each piece. Cut the sausages in half. Cut the tomatoes in half.

Trim off the ends of the mushrooms stems. Rinse the mushrooms, wiping off any dirt, and dry them on paper towels.

Thread all the prepared ingredients onto 4 skewers. Turn the broiler on high. Brush a little oil over the kabobs and cook them under the broiler for 5–8 minutes, until the sausages and bacon are browned on one side. Turn the kabobs over and cook the other side. Meanwhile, split and butter the bread rolls.

Have 4 plates ready. Turn off the heat and put 1 kabob on each plate. Garnish with watercress sprigs. Put a split and buttered bread roll on each plate and serve at once.

SUMMER GARDEN PARTY

Invite friends to a summer garden party or plan a little treat for the rest of the family. On really hot summer days people always used to wear hats to keep the sun off their heads. So, make your garden party a hat party. Tell your friends or the family they have to wear a hat.

THE BEST HATS

Have a prize for the best hat. Silly hats are easy to make. They can be made from colored paper with all sorts of bits and pieces glued on. Or a plain, old hat may be used as the base for a clever design. Add lots of flowers, bows or even artificial fruit to create a stunning hat!

THE HAT RACE

You will need 2 hats with ties sewn on. Divide the party into 2 teams. Each team has a hat. The teams stand in a line and the person at the front holds the hat. At the signal to 'go' the first person puts the hat on and ties it under their chin. Then he or she unties it and takes it off, quickly passing it to the next person. Everyone has to put the hat on, tie and untie it before passing it on. When the hat gets to the last person they tie the hat on and rush to the front. The first team to finish is the winner. Don't forget to have little prizes for the winners.

WHAT'S IN THE HAT?

This is a game for the family. Have a deep hat and put 6–10 things in it. Give every person a blindfold – a scarf to tie around their eyes will do. The hat full of things is passed around and every person has to decide what it contains by feeling the different objects. Each person is only allowed 1 minute to feel the bits and pieces. Ask everyone in turn if they can remember what was in the hat. The winner is the one who gets the most right. Find clever things to put in the hat: a flashlight, a bar of soap and so on.

WHAT TO PLAN

★ If you have just a few friends you may be able to sit around a table. If not have blankets out so you can sit on the lawn.
★ Plan some outdoor games – try some of the ideas for the Picnic Party (page 63). Pack and hide little gifts in the garden, then let your friends find them.
★ Remember to make a hat to wear.
★ Have 1 or 2 spare hats just in case someone forgets to bring their own.

Garden Party Menu
Ham Triangles
Stuffed Cucumber
Celery Boats
Strawberry Tartlets
Fruit Punch

ham triangles

¼ cup butter or margarine
8 thin slices bread
a little mustard
8 slices cooked ham
mustard and cress, to garnish

Makes 16

1 Place the butter in a bowl and soften with a spoon. Cut the crusts off the bread and spread with butter.

2 Spread 4 slices with a little mustard. Place a slice of ham on top, then put the remaining bread on top, buttered sides down, to make sandwiches.

3 Cut the sandwiches across into 4 triangles. Arrange these on a plate and cover with plastic wrap until you are ready to serve them. Put a few small bunches of mustard and cress around the sandwiches for garnish.

Stuffed Cucumber

8-inch piece cucumber
¼ cup soft cheese with garlic and herbs
½ cup cooked ham or boneless chicken
8 parsley sprigs

Makes 8 pieces

1 Peel the cucumber. Cut it into 8 slices measuring 1 inch thick. Use a teaspoon to scrape the middle out of the cucumbers. Do this carefully, taking out just the soft part with the seeds. Put a double thickness of paper towels on a plate and put the pieces of cucumber, cut sides down, on it to dry.

2 Put the soft cheese in a bowl. Cut the ham or chicken into thin strips. Cut the strips across into very small dice. Add the ham to the cheese and mix well.

3 Put a little of the cheese into each piece of cucumber. Use a teaspoon and a knife to push it into the hole in the middle of the cucumber. Place the stuffed cucumber on a plate and put a sprig of parsley on top.

Strawberry tartlets

1 quantity pastry dough
as for Mini Quiches (page 66)
2 tablespoons confectioners' sugar
1 teaspoon vanilla extract
1 pound strawberries
⅜ cup strawberry jam
1 tablespoon water

Makes 15

Set the oven at 400°F. Prepare all the ingredients for the pastry dough and make it following the recipe. Add the confectioners' sugar to the dry mixture when you have cut the fat into the flour. Add the vanilla extract with the water. Line 15 tartlet tins following the recipe.

Prick the pastry cases 2 or 3 times with a fork. Bake them for 10–15 minutes, until they are lightly browned. Set out a heatproof mat. Use pot holders to take the tins from the oven and then put it on the mat. Turn off the heat.

Leave the pastry cases in the tins for 5 minutes, then carefully lift them out using a spatula. Put them on a wire rack to cool.

Wash and dry the strawberries. Twist the stems and pull out the thin cores.

Put the jam in a bowl with the water. Put some water into a small saucepan and put it on the stove. Put the bowl on the saucepan and turn the heat to medium. Stir the jam until it has melted. Turn off the heat. Leave the bowl over the hot water.

Fill the tartlet cases with strawberries. Cut some of the strawberries in half if they are very big. Use pot holders to take the bowl of jam off the water. Brush the melted jam all over the strawberries in the tartlets. Leave to set before serving.

▶· celery boats ·◀

3 celery stalks
¼ pound cream cheese
a little paprika

Makes about 15

Trim the ends of the celery. Scrub the celery under cold water to remove all the dirt. Drain and dry on paper towels.

Cut the celery into 2-inch pieces. Put the cream cheese in a bowl and mix it with a spoon until it is soft.

Put a star tip into a pastry bag. Put the tip of the pastry bag into a jar, the fold the rest of the bag around the outside of the jar. Put the cream cheese into the bag.

Gather up the ends of the pastry bag and twist them together to enclose the cream cheese. Twist the ends of the bag together until the cream cheese is right down in the tip. Hold the tip over a piece of celery. Hold the celery with one hand and squeeze some cream cheese onto it in a neat line.

Pipe cream cheese onto all the celery pieces. Sprinkle just a little paprika on the tops. Arrange the Celery Boats on a plate. If you like put the celery and cucumber on the same plate.

▶· fruity punch ·◀

1 orange
1 lemon
2 tablespoons blackcurrant syrup
⅔ cup apple juice
1 large bottle sparkling mineral water

Makes 8 glasses

Prepare the orange and lemon the day before. Cut both into thin slices. Cover a small cookie sheet with plastic wrap and lay the slices on it. Put them in a freezer until they are hard.

Mix the blackcurrant syrup and apple juice in a pitcher. Pour in the mineral water. Add the frozen fruit slices. Leave for 5–10 minutes before serving. The frozen fruit slices cool the drink instead of ice cubes.

FINGER-LICKIN' LUNCH

Make lunch for the family or for your friends. This is a buffet lunch, so you can serve lots of bought snacks like nuts.

TABLE DECORATIONS

The type of decorations will depend on the time of year.

Spring – Have a yellow paper tablecloth, yellow napkins and bowls of fresh green and yellow ribbons. You can have pozies of miniature daffodils on the table. The Saturday before Easter is a good day to make a lunch treat. Put tiny baskets of miniature chocolate eggs on the table.

Summer – In summer put small pozies of flowers and huge bows on each corner of the table. Choose pink and pale green ribbons, and tie pretty bows with long ends. Use a pink or white paper table-cloth. Have pink and green paper napkins and arrange them in fans on the plates.

Autumn – Make small pozies of dried flowers. If you have a Hallowe'en lunch, put a hollowed out pumpkin with a face cut in it on the table. Stand a small candle in the pumpkin. Have rust, dark green and brown paper napkins and bows of ribbons in the same colors.

Winter – Decorate a winter table with bright red ribbon and pine cones. Add some fresh green ivy instead of pozies of flowers. Use bright red and green napkins with small bows of matching ribbons. For Christmas, add lots of holly, small balls and tinsel. If you have candle holders, put 1 or 2 candles on the table – they brighten up a dark winter day.

WHAT TO PLAN

Plan a simple indoor game that everyone will enjoy. For example, try charades. Everyone writes the name of a book, film, object, or animal on a piece of paper. The papers are folded and put in a bag. Everyone picks out a piece of paper. In turn, they mime whatever is written on their piece of paper. The others have to guess what was written on the paper.

Finger-lickin' Lunch Menu
Tuna Fish Dip
Cottage Cheese Dip (page 67)
Vegetable Dippers (page 67)
Potato chips and nuts
Pâté Toasts
Spicy Sausage Bites
Open Rolls
Easy Trifle
Homemade Lemonade

▶· Open rolls ·◀

4 4-inch bread rolls
¼ cup butter or margarine
4 cheese slices
24 slices cucumber

Makes 8

Split the rolls in half. Put the butter in a bowl and soften it with a spoon. Spread the butter or margarine on the rolls.

Cut the cheese slices in half. Cut each half into 3 pieces. Put 3 pieces of cheese and 3 slices of cucumber on each roll, overlapping them alternately.

Arrange the rolls on a plate and cover with plastic wrap until ready to serve.

▶· tuna fish dip ·◀

200 g/7 oz can tuna
100 g/4 oz soft cheese with herbs and garlic
6 tablespoons mayonnaise or natural yogurt
salt and pepper

Serves 6

Open the can of tuna and drain off the liquid. Put the tuna in a basin and mash it with a form until it is all broken into small shreds.

Add the soft cheese and mix well. Stir in the mayonnaise with salt and pepper to taste.

Put the dip in a dish. Cover with cling film and put it in the refrigerator until you are ready to put the food on the table.

▶· pâté toasts ·◀

¼ pound smooth pâté
12 Melba toasts
3–4 radishes
12 parsley sprigs

Makes 12

If the pâté is firm, put it in a bowl and soften it by beating with a wooden spoon. Carefully spread the pâté on the Melba toasts. Do this flat on a board. The Melba toasts will break if you try to spread the pâté on them on a plate.

Cut the radishes into thin slices. Arrange some slices of radish and a sprig of parsley on each Pâté Toast. Put the Pâté Toasts on a plate and cover with plastic wrap until ready to serve.

1

2

▸· spicy sausage bites ·◂

1 Cut the sausages into 4 pieces. Put the curry powder in a large bowl. Crush the garlic in a garlic crusher over the bowl. Scrape all the bits from the outside of the crusher.

2 Add the tomato catchup, yogurt or lemon juice to the curry powder. Sprinkle in a little salt and pepper. Put the pieces of sausage in the bowl and mix well with a spoon. Carry on mixing up the sausages until all the pieces are flavored with the curry paste.

3 Put a skillet pan on the stovetop. Add the oil and turn the heat to medium. After 1 minute the oil will be hot and it will run freely over the pan if you tilt it. Add all the sausages. Cook for 15–20 minutes, stirring the sausages often so they brown all over.

4 Put a double thickness of paper towels in a bowl. Turn off the heat. Tip all the sausages onto the paper. Shake the paper a little, then leave the sausages to cool.

5 Drain the onions. Thread each piece of sausage onto a toothpick with an onion. Put all the bites on a plate or stick them into a grapefruit.

8 skinless link sausages
1 teaspoon curry powder
1 clove garlic
1 tablespoon tomato catchup
1 tablespoon plain yogurt or lemon juice
salt and pepper
1 tablespoon vegetable oil
1 small jar cocktail onions
1 grapefruit (optional)

Makes 32

▸· homemade lemonade ·◂

2 large lemons
scant 1 cup sugar
4 tablespoons water
1 large bottle sparkling mineral water
ice cubes
lemon slices, to serve (optional)

Makes 8 glasses

1 Grate the peel off both lemons on a fine grater. Put the peel in a saucepan. Cut the lemons in half and squeeze out all their juice. Add this to the pan.

2 Add the sugar and water to the pan. Put the pan on the stovetop and turn the heat to medium. Cook, stirring until the sugar has dissolved completely. Turn off the heat. Leave the lemon syrup to cool.

3 Put the cold syrup in a pitcher. Top up with mineral water. Add ice cubes and lemon slices if you like.

▶· easy cherry trifle ·◀

1 large jelly roll
3 tablespoons orange juice
15-ounce can cherry pie filling
15-ounce can Bird's custard
⅔ cup heavy cream
¼ cup slivered almonds
6–8 maraschino or candied cherries
6–8 small strips angelica

Serves 4–6

Cut the jelly roll into thin slices. Put them in the bottom of a glass and about a third of the way up the side. Put any extra slices in a second layer. Sprinkle the orange juice over the jelly roll. Open the can of pie filling and use a spoon to spread it evenly over the jelly roll.

Open the can of custard and pour it into a bowl, scraping all the custard out of the can. Put the cream in a basin and use a whisk to whip it until it stands in soft peaks. Add all the cream to the custard. Use a spatula to scrape the basin. Use a large metal spoon to fold the cream into the custard. Spread this all over the cherry pie filling.

Put the trifle in the refrigerator for at least 1 hour, better still, leave it overnight. Heat the broiler to high. Put a piece of foil on the broiler rack and sprinkle the almonds on it. Brown the almonds under the broiler. Watch them all the time as they burn very easily. Use a long-handled wooden spoon to turn them once or twice. Turn the broiler off and leave the almonds to cool.

Sprinkle the almonds over the trifle. Stick a small piece of angelica into each cherry. Arrange the cherries around the trifle just before serving it.

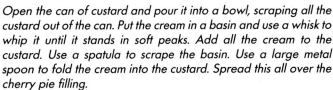

A Gift From The Cook

▸· special dates and walnuts ·◂

1   Use a small pointed knife to make a cut down the length of each date. Carefully pick out the pits from the middle of the dates.

2   Take a small teaspoon and put a little of the cream cheese into each date. Take care not to make a mess on the outside of the dates. Spread the remaining cheese on the flat side of 6 of the walnuts. Press the other 6 walnut halves onto the cheese.

6 dates
12 walnut halves
3 ounces cream cheese with herbs and garlic

Makes 12

3   Put the dates and walnuts in paper candy cases and pack them in a small box. Cover with plastic wrap and store in the refrigerator.

▸· stilton bites ·◂

1   Put the cheese in a bowl and mash it with a fork until it is reduced to small crumbs. Add the butter use a spoon to mix it with the cheese. Beat the mixture until it is soft. Tip the flour into the bowl and stir it into the cheese mixture to make a soft dough. Use a knife to mark the dough in half, then into quarters.

2   Grease a cookie sheet. From each quarter of the dough you should roll 3 balls. Put the balls on the cookie sheet, well apart. Flatten each ball slightly and press a blanched almond on top. Put the cookie sheet in the refrigerator for 30 minutes to chill the cheese balls.

3   Set the oven at 400°F. Bake the cheese balls for 15–20 minutes, until they are golden. Have a heatproof mat ready. Set out a wire rack. Use pot holders to take the cookie sheet from the oven. Use a spatula to lift the Stilton Bites off the sheet and put them on the wire rack to cool. Turn off the oven.

½ cup crumbled Stilton cheese
¼ cup butter
¾ cup all-purpose flour
12 blanched almonds

Makes 12

4   When they are cold, pack the Stilton Bites in a box or very small basket. Line the container with a paper napkin and cover with plastic wrap.

▶ peanut crunch ◀

1 cup heaped sugar
⅔ cup water
1 cup salted peanuts
2 tablespoons butter
¼ teaspoon baking soda

Makes a 7-inch square

1 Put the sugar in a saucepan. Pour in the water. Put the pan on the stove. Now prepare all the other ingredients before cooking.

2 Have the peanuts near the stove ready to add to the caramel. Put the butter on a small saucer near the stove. Put the baking soda in its measuring spoon on a saucer near the stove. Lastly, grease a 7-inch square baking pan. Stand the pan on a wooden board.

3 Turn the heat to medium and stir the sugar and water until the sugar has dissolved completely. Do not stir the syrup again. Turn the heat to high and bring the syrup to the boil. Turn the heat down slightly but keep the syrup boiling and bubbling rapidly.

4 Watch the syrup all the time but do not stir it. After a while it will begin to change color, turning very pale brown. Once it begins to turn brown it will brown quickly.

5 When it is a light golden color (like syrup) turn off the heat. Add all the peanuts, butter and baking soda. Stir quickly to mix the nuts into the caramel. The baking soda will make it frothy.

6 Pour the mixture into the greased pan. Scrape it all out of the pan. Put the pan in the sink and fill it with water otherwise it will be difficult to wash.

7 Leave the mixture until it is completely cold and hard. Break it into chunks with the handle of a wooden spoon. Pack the chunks in a plastic bag and put an airtight clip on them.

HELP POINT
Boiling sugar syrup is tricky and it can be dangerous. Always make sure you have an adult with you.

hazelnut truffles

Simple Coffee Cake truffles

6 squares chocolate
¼ cup unsalted butter
½ cup toasted chopped skinned hazelnuts
1 tablespoon orange juice
1 tablespoon light cream or fromage frais
cocoa powder for coating

Makes about 20

4 squares chocolate
2 cups plain cake crumbs
2 teaspoons instant coffee
2 tablespoons boiling water
chocolate strands for coating

Makes about 20

1 Break the chocolate into pieces and put them in a heatproof bowl. Add the butter. Pour some water into a small saucepan and put it on the stove. Turn the heat to medium.

2 Stand the bowl over the saucepan of water. Stir the chocolate and butter until both are completely melted. Do not allow the water to boil up at all. Turn the heat to low if the water begins to boil.

3 Turn off the heat and use pot holders to lift the bowl off the saucepan. Stir in the hazelnuts and orange juice. Leave the mixture to cool for about 30 minutes.

4 Stir the cream or fromage frais into the chocolate, then put the bowl in the refrigerator until the chocolate is firm enough to shape into balls. This will take about 45 minutes. It can be left for longer, then allowed to stand at room temperature for a while to soften slightly.

5 Put a small pile of cocoa on a plate. Set out about 20 paper candy cases. Wash your hands under cold water and dry them. Try to keep your hands cold while you roll the truffles to stop you getting into a sticky mess!

6 Take a teaspoonful of the mixture and drop it on the cocoa. Roll it quickly into a ball and put it in a paper candy case. Shape all the remaining truffles then put them in the refrigerator for at least 1 hour before packing them in a box. Cover with plastic wrap. Add a bow and a tag.

Break the chocolate into squares and put them in a bowl. Pour some water into a small saucepan and put it on the stovetop. Stand the bowl over the water. Turn the heat to medium. Stir the chocolate until it melts. Turn the heat to low if the water begins to boil.

Turn off the heat and use pot holders to lift the bowl off the pan. Put the cake in a bowl.

Put the cake in a bowl. Wash and dry your hands. Crumble the cake with your fingertips until it is all in tiny crumbs.

Put the coffee in a cup and add the boiling water. Stir well. Use a teaspoon to sprinkle this coffee all over the cake. Pour the melted chocolate over the cake. Scrape all the chocolate out of the bowl.

Use a spoon to mix the cake with the chocolate and coffee. Stir it for some time until it is all really well mixed up.

Put a small pile of chocolate strands on a plate. Set out about 20 paper candy cases on a cookie sheet. Wash and dry your hands again.

Take small spoonfuls of the mixture and shape it into balls. Roll the balls in the chocolate strands, then put them into paper cases. Put the truffles in the refrigerator for at least 1 hour before you pack them in a box and cover with plastic wrap. Add a bow and a tag.

·►·quick peppermint creams·◄·

a little confectioners' sugar
½ pound packet fondant cake frosting
(frosting to roll out)
peppermint extract
green food coloring

Makes about 30

1 Set out a small cookie sheet. Lay a sheet of plastic wrap on it and sprinkle confectioners' sugar over.

2 Place just a little confectioners' sugar on the counter-top. Unwrap the frosting and knead it lightly into a smooth ball. Dip a toothpick into the peppermint extract and dab it onto the frosting. Knead it again. Do this until all the frosting is flavored with peppermint. Add more extract if needed.

3 Cut the piece of frosting in half. Wrap one half in plastic wrap and set aside. Cut the other piece into about 15 equal lumps. Roll each lump into a smooth ball, then flatten it into a smooth circle.

4 Dip your fingertip in a little confectioners' sugar. Rub the side and top of the candy very gently with your fingertip to make it smooth and shiny. Place on the cookie sheet. Roll and flatten the other white candies.

5 Unwrap the other piece of frosting. Dip a toothpick into the green food coloring and drop just a little onto the frosting. Knead it until it is all evenly pale green. Shape into candies like you did with the white frosting.

6 Leave the Peppermint Creams to dry for 2–3 hours. Put them into paper candy cases, then place them in a box and cover with plastic wrap. Add a bow.

HELP POINT
Take care not to add too much green colouring. Just add a drop at a time or the colour will be too dark.

ᴵ►· *chocolate fruits* ·◄ᴵ

These are fun to make and they taste really good. You may use different sorts of fruit. Here are some fruits you may like to try:

*green grapes on their stems
strawberries with stems
cherries with stems
segments of mandarin orange*

1 Use dark semi-sweet chocolate, milk chocolate or white chocolate. It is best to melt too much chocolate so it is easy to dip the fruit. Leave any leftover chocolate in the bowl until it hardens, then take it out, wrap it in plastic wrap and keep it in the refrigerator until next time.

2 Gently wash the fruit and dry it on paper towels. Lay a sheet of waxed paper on a cookie sheet and put it near the stove.

3 Have all the fruit for dipping on a large plate. Break some chocolate (8 squares) into squares and place them in a heatproof bowl.

4 Put some water into a saucepan and put it on the stovetop. Stand the bowl over the water and turn the heat to medium. Stir the chocolate until it has dissolved completely. Lower the heat if the water begins to boil.

5 Use pot holders to lift the bowl off the pan. Pick up a piece of fruit and dip it into the chocolate so it is half covered. Lift it out and let the excess chocolate drip back into the bowl. Give the fruit a gentle twist and put it on the paper-lined cookie sheet.

6 When all the fruit is dipped leave the chocolate to set completely before placing them in paper candy cases. If you prefer, put the fruits in a small dish without the paper cases. Cover with plastic wrap.

ᴵ►·*marzipan fruits* ·◄ᴵ

*225g/8 oz marzipan (white marzipan is best)
red, green, yellow and orange food colourings
a few cloves*

Makes about 24

1 Wash and dry your hands. Put a sheet of plastic wrap on a cookie sheet. Get all the food colors and a very fine paint brush ready.

2 Knead the marzipan until it is soft. Break off a small piece and roll it into a ball. Mold the ball into a thin sausage shape to look like a banana. Curve it slightly and flatten it along one side. Make a very tiny stem shape at one end. Put the banana on the cookie sheet.

3 To shape a strawberry, roll out a piece of marzipan into a ball, then mold a pointed end and flatten the opposite end. Make a very small, flat circle of marzipan and cut it all round the edge into points to look like strawberry leaves. Brush a tiny drop of water on the leaves and stick it on the flat end of the fruit.

4 Shaping oranges is easy. Just roll out some marzipan into a ball and flatten the top slightly. Make an apple in the same way, molding it with a slightly flatter top.

5 When you are molding the fruit put the same types near each other on the tray. Paint them with food coloring. Paint just 1 color at a time.

6 Paint the bananas yellow, the strawberries red, the strawberry leaves and the apples green and the orange with orange coloring. Wash and dry the brush before starting a new color.

7 Now add the features to the fruit. Use a very tiny grater (one used for grating nutmeg) to mark the skin on the oranges. Use a toothpick to mark the dents in the strawberries. Mark small creases around the top of the apple using a toothpick.

8 When the colors are dry, use brown coloring to paint fine lines on the banana and paint the stem. Leave the fruits overnight.

9 Put the fruits in paper candy cases and pack them in a box. Cover with plastic wrap.

⊪►· sweet popcorn ·◄⫿

2 tablespoons vegetable oil
2 tablespoons popping corn
2 tablespoons sugar

Makes 1 bag

1 You will need a fairly large saucepan which has a lid. Have a heatproof bowl ready to hold the cooked popcorn. Pour the oil into the pan and put it on the stovetop. Heat the oil over medium heat for about 2 minutes.

2 Add all the corn to the pan and put the lid on. Turn the heat to high until the corn begins to pop. When the corn is popping turn the heat to the lowest setting. Shake the pan occasionally and cook the corn until the popping has stopped.

POPCORN SPECIALS

★ *Popcorn is good savory as well as sweet. Do not add the sugar. Instead, add a knob of butter and 2 tablespoons of grated Parmesan cheese to the corn and stir for about 1 minute. Sprinkle with a little salt and paprika, then leave to cool.*

★ *Instead of sugar, trickle 2 tablespoons honey over the popcorn and stir for a few seconds until the corn is golden. Turn into the bowl to cool.*

★ *Mix the cold corn with raisins and nuts to make a bag of mixed snacks.*

3 Use pot holders to lift the lid off the pan. Sprinkle the sugar over the popcorn and stir well. Turn the heat to a high setting and stir the corn until the sugar melts and browns. This should take less than a minute. Take care not to overcook the popcorn or the sugar will burn.

4 When the corn is lightly browned and beginning to stick together, turn it all into the bowl and leave it until it is cold. Do not taste the popcorn until it is cold because the caramelized sugar is very hot.

5 Pour cold water into the saucepan to soak otherwise the sugar hardens on it. Pack the cold popcorn in a plastic bag and seal it with a metal tie. Tie ribbon and a tag on the bag.

⊩·toffee apples·◁⊢

4 red apples
4 wooden skewers
1 cup sugar
⅔ cup water

Makes 4

Wash and thoroughly dry the apples, then polish them with paper towels until they shine. Place a piece of waxed paper on a cookie sheet. Stick a wooden skewer into the core of each apple and stand them on the cookie sheet.

Put the sugar in a saucepan. Pour in the water. Put the pan on the stovetop. Turn the heat to medium and stir the sugar and water until the sugar has dissolved completely. Do not stir the syrup again. Turn the heat to high and bring the syrup to the boil. Turn the heat down slightly but keep the syrup boiling and bubbling rapidly.

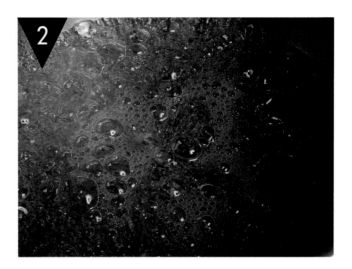

Watch the syrup all the time but do not stir it. After a while it will begin to change color, turning very pale brown. Once it begins to turn brown it will brown quickly.

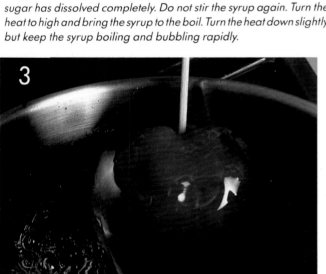

When it is a light golden color (like syrup) turn the heat off. Hold the apples by their sticks and dip them quickly in the caramel. Tilt the pan slightly if necessary to coat the apples and twist them around.

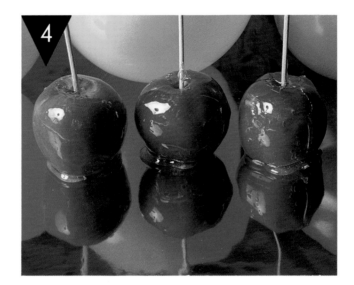

Let the excess caramel drip off back into the bowl, then twist each apple to catch the last of the drips and put it back on the cookie sheet. Leave until the caramel is cold and hard. Do not keep the apples longer than 2 days or they become very sticky.

INDEX

A

Angelica leaves 47
Apple(s):
    and Cheese on Toast
      26
    and Sausage Filler 61
    Toffee 95

B

Bacon:
    Kabob 80
    and Salad Croissant
      60
    Toasted Sandwich 57
Baked Beans: 45
    Bean Feast 26
    with Baked Potatoes
      25
Banana:
    Date Logs 16
    Muffins 33
    Splits 41
Barbecue-style Vegi
    Burgers 53
Bean Feast 26
Beany Potatoes 25
Birthday Cake,
    Jammy 17
Biscuits, Simple 31
Breadcrumbs,
    making 9
Brownies 32
Burger:
    Barbecue-style Vegi
      53
    Salad 52

C

Carrot Cake, One-
    stage 77
Celery Boats 83
Cheese:
    and Apple on Toast
      26
    Cottage Cheese Dip
      67
    Cream Cheese
      Frosting 77
    Mini Quiches 66
    Rainbow Sputnik 12
    Sandwich Supper 46
    Savories 13
    Sesame Cheese Puffs
      28
    Simple Biscuits 31
    Special Dates and
      Walnuts 88
    Stilton Bites 88
    Toasted Sandwich 57
Cheesecake, Lemon
    Jelly 75

Cherries, Hidden 19
Chicken:
    Corn Chowder 55
    Noodles 54
    Stock 42
Chocolate:
    Choc-chip Ice Cream
      21
    Cookies 69
    Crunch Munch 14
    Fruits 92
    Milk Shakes 71
    No-cook Chocolate
      Fudge Tart 49
    Orange Fingers 18
    Yogurt Swirl 37
Coconut Cookie
    Cake 47
Coffee Cake Truffles,
    Simple 90
Coleslaw Cups 27
Cookies:
    Basic 69
    Clever 15
    Coconut Cookie
      Cake 47
    Peanut 70
    Pinwheel 71
Corned Beef:
    Hash-tash 55
    Toasted Sandwich 57
Cottage Cheese Dip
    67
Cream Cheese
    Frosting 77
Crazy Crackers 11
Crunch Munch 14
Crunchy Hot Orange
    29
Cucumber, Stuffed
    82

D

Dates:
    Banana Date Logs 16
    Special Walnuts and
      88
Doughnut Dessert 43

E

Eggs:
    Nutty 22
    separating 9
    Taco Tomato
      Scramble 58

F

Fish Stick Quiche 44–5
Fish-topped Fingers
    26

Fishy Filling,
    Potatoes with 24
Flapjacks, Orange 32
Flour, rubbing fat
    into 9
Fruit(s):
    Chocolate 92
    Frosted 20
    Marzipan 93
    Tropical Desserts 35
Fruit Salad, Nutty 30
Fruity Punch 83

G

Garlic Bread 74
Golden Baked Potatoes
    24
Grapefruit Cocktails 80

H

Ham:
    Sandwich Supper 46
    Topping with
      Potatoes 25
    Tostada Toppers 59
    Triangles 82
Hash-tash 55
Hazelnut Truffles 90
Hot Dog Kabobs 50
Hot Dog Tostada
    Toppers 59

I

Ice Cream:
    Choc-chip 21
    Peach Melba 78

J

Jelly:
    Lemon Jelly
      Cheesecake 75
    Tropical Desserts 35

K

Kabobs:
    Bacon 80
    Hot Dog 50

L

Lemon Jelly Cheesecake
    75
Lemonade, Homemade
    86

M

Marmalade Pears 39
Marzipan: 10
    Carrots 77
    Fruits 93
    Hidden Cherries 19
Meatballs, Mini 64
Milk Shakes, Chocolate
    71
Muffins, Banana 33
Mushrooms, cleaning 9

N

No-cook Chocolate
    Fudge Tart 49
Noodles, Chicken 54
Nutty Eggs 22
Nutty Fruit Salad 30

O

Onions, how to chop 8
Open Rolls 85
Orange:
    Chocolate Orange
      Fingers 18
    Crunchy Hot 29
    Flapjacks 32

P

Parsley, chopping 35
Pasta:
    Cover Up 51
    Pronto 34
Pastacular 48
Pâté Toasts 85
Peach Melba 78
Peanut Cookies 70
Peanut Crunch 89
Peanut Rarebit 26
Pears, Marmalade 39
Peppermint Creams,
    Quick 91
Pinwheel Cookies 71
Pizza 36
Pizza Sticks 65
Pizza Topping 26
Popcorn, Sweet 94
Pork Toasted Sandwich
    57
Pork 'n' Potato Loaf 40
Potatoes: 23–5
    Beany 25
    with Creamy Ham
      Topping 25
    with Fishy Fillings 24
    Golden Baked 24
    Pork 'n' Potato Loaf
      40
    Red Hot Baked 23

Q

Quiches, Mini 66

R

Rainbow Rice 42
Rainbow Sputnik 12
Rainbow Veg 39
Red Hot Baked Potatoes
    23
Rice Cocktails 45
Rice, Rainbow 42

S

St Clement's Cookies 69
Salad:
    and Bacon Croissant
      60

Burger 52
Coleslaw Cups 27
Nutty Fruit 30
Spectacular 37
Tomato 47
Salami Stick Roll-up 56
Salami Tostada Toppers
    59
Sandwich, Toasted 57
Sandwich Rolls 65
Sandwich Supper 46
Sausage and Apple Filler
    61
Sausage Bites, Spicy 86
Savory Rolls 72
Sesame Cheese Puffs 28
Soup Special, Quick 62
Stilton Bites 88
Stir-fry Vegetables 41
Strawberry Tartlets 82

T

Taco Tomato Scramble
    58
Tea, Iced 78
Toast Toppers 26
Toasted Sandwiches 57
Toasts, Pâté 85
Toffee Apples 95
Tomato Salad 47
Tomato Scramble, Taco
    58
Tomatoes, Stuffed 73
Tostada Toppers 59
Trifle, Easy Cherry 87
Tropical Desserts 35
Truffles:
    Hazelnut 90
    Simple Coffee Cake
      90
Tuna:
    Crunch 38
    Fish Dip 85
    Rarebit Rolls 57
    Toasted Sandwich 57

V

Vegetables:
    Dipper 67
    Rainbow Veg 39
    Stir-fry 41
Vegi Burger, Barbecue-
    style 53

W

Walnut Biscuits 69
Walnuts and Dates,
    Special 88

Y

Yogurt Fizz 80
Yogurt Swirl, Chocolate
    37